I0819442

flower energy

# flower energy

channeling the healing power of blooms

JENNY BARKER
the FLOWER DOCTOR

RUNNING PRESS
PHILADELPHIA

Running Press
Hachette Book Group
1290 Avenue of the Americas, New York, NY 10104
www.runningpress.com
@Running_Press

First Edition: March 2026

Published by Running Press, an imprint of Hachette Book Group, Inc. The Running Press name and logo are trademarks of Hachette Book Group, Inc.



Print book cover and interior design by Susan Van Horn

Library of Congress Control Number: 2025003441

ISBNs: 978-0-7624-8906-0 (hardcover), 978-0-7624-8907-7 (ebook)

Printed in China

1010

10 9 8 7 6 5 4 3 2 1

for Jack Golden

# contents

# preface

Flowers wrote this book. I'm just the vehicle to share their story.

You might wonder how this book came to be. During one of my last visits with my dad, before he passed away, we were sitting on the patio and he said, "You're going to write a book." When he told me this prophecy, I thought he'd lost his mind. In fact, I was so triggered by his prediction that I didn't see him again for a while. You see, I dropped out of college and hated school in general. The thought of sitting down to write an essay, much less a book, was a ridiculous proposition, so much so that it felt like my dad was mocking me.

I finally went back to visit again after receiving a call from a nurse, who let me know he wasn't doing well. I was still bothered and bewildered by his last comment and was hoping he had forgotten it. Of course, he remembered. He looked at me and said again, "About that book . . ." I wanted to put my hand up in front of him like a stop sign, but because he was fragile and quickly deteriorating, I resisted. He continued: "The way you're going to be seen is by writing this book." I told him that I don't write, and I reminded him that I dropped out of school because I didn't like writing papers. He was persistent: "You're going to write this book by picking up the phone and telling a good story." I looked at him and smiled, and that's when I had my light bulb moment. I *am* really good at telling stories. *I can do it*, I thought to myself.

This book is filled with stories of my life: running a flower shop, being a mom, and showing up for my son and my clients. In these pages you will read about the flower shop itself, which I have created with purpose and intention, where music is flowing and the staff is energized to jump in to assist. It's pure joy for me to share with my customers–and now you, the reader–the messages embedded in the flowers. Since I realized my gift and secret powers, which I will tell you more about in the pages to come, I have accessed my ability to stay open to messages that I hear: The flowers tell me a story, and I am present to listen. I've shared these messages with thousands of clients. They aren't shocked or even surprised by what I reveal, because the messages are intuitive and accurate.

I have learned that flowers are the best medicine. I am known as the Flower Doctor because I prescribe flowers to make people feel good and to bring joy, happiness, and laughter to people's lives. I try to see the positive in every situation. There were times in my life when things really sucked–my boyfriend was unfaithful, or my employee lost a huge order, or I got a ticket for driving too fast–but I always tried and I continue to try to stay focused on the blessing of how I can improve myself and learn from difficult situations.

I want this book to feel like you've walked into my store in Redondo Beach, California, two blocks from the ocean, like you've been welcomed into my life and my world. The next time you look at a flower, I want you to feel its power and think of all the magical stories each bloom tells.

# introduction

## *A room with flowers is a room with life.*

Do you know how magical it is to wake up every day and to be of service, bringing beauty and joy to as many people as possible through fresh flowers? People come from all over to visit my store—regular clients of twenty-five years and first-time visitors in town from Germany, Russia, Ireland, and beyond. I try to explain to people how flowers help benefit a relationship or transform a person's life. My mission is to bring smiles everywhere I go and to create a flower movement.

Flowers tell a story. They have a life of their own. They are transformative. They can bring cheer to a celebration, joy to a new life, and comfort to grief or pain.

Flowers, in their living and breathing state, have something to say, and I'm their vessel for sharing those messages. Touching a million flowers and spending thousands of hours studying them might seem overwhelming, but not to me. I'm obsessed with flowers. No matter what I'm going through in life—the highs, the lows, the turbulence—the one thing that has helped me get through it all is flowers. If I have flowers next to me, I'm safe and I know that I'm going to be okay. Flowers keep you company and give off a sense of calm. They are so powerful.

When I was going through a divorce, I depended on my team. I'm not talking about

therapists or counselors; I'm talking about my team of flowers, which offered a lifeline by offering a support system of nature and beauty. I was heartbroken, but as a single mom, I had to show up for my son and my business. I leaned heavily on the healing effects of flowers and truly began to see how instrumental they are for those in need.

Each flower is a unique piece of artwork, whether a rose, marigold, kangaroo paws, lisianthus, smilax, dahlia, or celosia (cockscomb). Mother Nature has created this unique bloom, and she decides its shape, color, and texture—and even the season when it shows up in our lives. You can see the beauty and the uniqueness in each stem. Each flower is alive and represents a beautiful soul. The reason we give flowers to others is to remind them of this beauty. Flowers are like a heartbeat—they hold energy and act as an emotional support system. They are also a pure reflection of Mother Nature's artistry.

ABOVE, CLOCKWISE FROM TOP LEFT: Marigold, lisianthus, kangaroo paw, coxcomb, amaranthus. • OPPOSITE: Marigolds.

## My Grandpa's Garden

I grew up in Redondo Beach, California, and was raised by a single mom. I have one brother, who is three years older than me. My mother worked full time as a journalist at the local newspaper, and my maternal grandparents took care of me and my brother while she worked. We were always at my grandparents' house—it was my favorite place in the world. My grandpa was British, and his garden was his pride and joy. It was a traditional English garden filled with beautiful flowers. I spent many hours admiring them. In his proper British accent, he would always ask me, referring to his roses, "Do you like them?" When he would pick me up at school, he would bring roses cut fresh from his garden to give to the librarian. He was not being flirtatious. He was just all about sharing the beauty of his garden with other people, and that instinct rubbed off on me.

I saw the joy that the flowers brought my grandfather, and that inspired me. I loved walking barefoot on the grass. I remember feeling the blades under my feet and thinking how connected I felt to Mother Earth. My grandpa adored tending to the gardens on weekends, and I was mesmerized watching him. His exquisite rosebushes and beautiful bougainvillea, with their phases of growth and hypnotic fragrance, put me under their spell.

I would visit the roses and smell each one. My grandpa would ask me which was my favorite that day. It was usually the purple ones, since they were the most fragrant, but sometimes the ugliest rose called to me. I was always surprised by the powerful floral fragrance that a rose gave off, even when it was not yet fully bloomed. When it opened, I felt a new appreciation and respect for its beauty. Later on in life, I learned that flowers could make me feel good even in the ugliest situations.

I admired the depth and transformation of the roses: They would start as a colorless bud, and then, a few days later, the rose would begin to show its true colors. In the spiritual realm, the rose is associated with the heart chakra and is considered a healer. If you're trying to open your heart, heal your heart, or speak from your

heart, put a rose anywhere on your body, and the flower's energy will vibrate to the heart. Shamans and healers use this practice to heal and spiritually connect to the heart.

It was in my grandpa's garden that I remember feeling the energy of flowers for the first time—my first tangible step in seeing the world refracted through their energy. I would sit with the flowers like Buddha in silence. I would stare at them and pick up on their emotions and their shape, texture, and scent. I would zone in on the distinct architecture of each flower. I found that if I sat with the flower and stared at it and came to complete silence, it would send me a message.

I thought I wanted to be a decorator when I grew up. When I was little, I played with my Barbie and pretended to sell things and ring people up in my pretend store. I knew I wanted to be a powerful businesswoman who was recognized professionally. I didn't picture myself married, and I wasn't thinking about having kids. I wanted to live in a high-rise condo in New York City. I studied details in homes, buildings, and landscaping. I was obsessed with flowers—on every surface. I wanted to drink out of a beautiful floral cup. The plate I used had to have flowers on it, and so must the wallpaper, the pillows, and so on. Flowers made me smile and feel good inside my body. I vibe with flowers.

At a young age, I would walk into a room and notice something was missing. I knew when a room needed a little bit of life. I would go outside and ask my grandpa to let me cut

**OPPOSITE:** Tea roses, stock, lilac, pink jasmine, bridal veil broom, burning bush, larkspur.

some flowers, and then I would find a vase in the cupboard and fill it with water. I'd put greenery and flowers in the vase—I noticed that if I mixed flowers with greenery and chose different colors, it would bring more harmony to the space, and I could change the emotional frequency of the room. Brighter, bolder colors were able to increase the serotonin in the brain, while more somber colors created feelings of peace and calm. I would figure out where in the room I wanted to place the energy of the flowers and display them. I would set flowers in each room of the house—an acknowledgment of my presence, a statement that I had been in the room. Leaving flowers behind meant that I was bringing my excitement and energy into those spaces, as well as the range of emotions that flowers can provide. I was able to decorate a room at a young age by only using flowers.

FLOWER℞

**Total support system.** *Lighter tones (white, pinks, and purples). Stock, roses, lisianthus.*

## Finding My Calling

When I was fifteen, I worked in a bakery, and there was a flower shop across the street that would barter with us, exchanging flowers for baked goods. After the florist dropped off the flowers, I would arrange and display them on the tables. I soon realized that I would much rather be working in the flower shop than in the bakery. One Saturday, after working a ten-hour shift, I walked across the street to the flower shop to ask if they were hiring. They weren't, but instead of taking no for an answer, I kept bugging them. I would come in every week and ask if they needed help. I used my meager paycheck to buy flowers from the shop. I kept showing up every week—I even said I would be willing to take out their trash. They finally hired me, and that's how I got my start in the flower business.

The flower shop was called The Arrangement, and it was on the Pacific Coast Highway, just one block away from my home and located in a very bright Barbie-pink building. You couldn't miss it. When I started working there, I quickly discovered that most of our clients would come in the door for one of a few reasons: They were in a rush and needed last-minute flowers for an event; they were looking for a gift for a birthday, anniversary, or some other celebration; or they were seeking forgiveness for something. They would always ask for my input, and I felt pretty cool about being their flower expert. I was very good at problem-solving, but more important, I thrived on trying to make people feel better by channeling the energy of the flowers.

I loved going to work. I felt independent and proud to be behind the counter taking orders and making beautiful designs. I was purposely creating joy to transform a customer's mood while at the same time uplifting my own mood.

Being at work felt like a vacation. I loved talking to and helping customers and making my own money, because that meant I could buy my own clothes and food and go to the movies. I could afford life. I loved that I could also be of service and that customers appreciated me. I felt completely present in the flower shop. I was making life better for others. Designing with flowers was a dream for me.

I delighted in coming to work wearing a cute flowing flowered dress and hat. I would tie on an apron and get ready for my shift. On my second day of work in the flower shop, the owner left me in charge while he ran errands. I was alone in the shop when a stretch limousine pulled up and a frazzled-looking man in a tuxedo stepped out and sprinted into the shop. He told me he was getting married that day and the florist didn't show up, so his wife had no bouquet. I sprang into action and created a simple yet stunning bouquet for his wife-to-be. He was so appreciative and even tipped me $100. From that moment, I was hooked. It was validation that I had an eye and a deep understanding of how flowers should be handled, designed, and enjoyed.

Looking back, I realize that this was when I discovered my life's purpose. With zero training and by using my interior design skills and intuition, I became the youngest designer in the flower shop. Most designers went to school and

FLOWERx

**For a best friend.**
*Darker pink tones. Snapdragons, ranunculus, lisianthus, roses, mint, gunni eucalyptus.*

worked their way up from cleaning coolers and buckets and only after maybe a year or more of that started to design. I was a floral designer from the beginning. I knew that this was what I was supposed to do. I was not meant to be out in the world, working in an office, away from nature. I'm meant to be of service, bringing beauty and joy everywhere.

There I was, only fifteen years old, essentially running a flower shop. We didn't have smartphones in 1995, so to educate myself, I kept a pocket-sized flower guidebook with accompanying photographs in my apron to learn the names of each flower. When the flowers arrived in the shop, I would put a name card on each bucket to help me memorize them. Being able to fire off the names of the flowers to customers boosted my confidence.

The owner started to give me more responsibility with events. I couldn't wait to get to work after school. Soon clients started requesting my floral designs. The owner noticed this, and he gave me raises. By the time I was eighteen, I was earning $25 an hour. Back in 1998, that was a lot, considering minimum wage at the time was $4.25.

Around this time, I was graduating from high school. I was eighteen years old, and my mom decided it was time for me to be independent. I moved into a dream apartment on the Esplanade. I had to earn my own money, so I got two jobs. Emotionally and spiritually, I felt like I could spread my wings and fly, but I needed to learn how to support myself and figure out how to pay my bills on my own. Handling independent adulthood was a learning curve. It was hard, but at the same time, I knew I could make it. Before I knew it, I began to see the rewards for all my efforts.

I wanted to go to college, but I didn't take the SATs and I was never encouraged to focus on homework or to get good grades, so I was left with few choices for higher education. I enrolled in Santa Monica City College and quit the flower shop. I found a job closer to my school as a hostess at a super-trendy celebrity hotspot called Santa Monica Seafood. At my new job, I noticed the restaurant needed flowers to create a beautiful ambience for diners to enjoy, so I offered to provide and arrange the flowers at cost. The owners loved the flowers very much, and my boss encouraged me to create arrangements for his three other restaurants. Diners were asking who designed the flowers, too.

I was close with my high school sweetheart Zeke's family. His was a Jewish home, and I loved his parents, Mali and Brian. They treated me like I was their child. One day, Mali sat me down and said, "Jenny, you should start your own business." I thought she was crazy to believe I could start my own business. At the time, I was living in a one-bedroom apartment on the best block in Redondo Beach, Esplanade, on the west side. I could hear waves crashing from my bedroom, and my garage overlooked the ocean. I manifested this spot. Although I was barely making enough to pay rent, I somehow managed to swing it every month. I reminded myself of my dad's encouragement and faith in me, and I decided to embrace Mali's suggestion rather than question it.

With Mali's support and guidance, I took the plunge. I knew how to arrange flowers because I had worked at the flower shop for three years, I was creating flower designs for multiple restaurants, and I had built up a small private client list. I didn't know anything about business or accounting or spreadsheets, but I did know how to wow people with my flowers. The restaurant job paid well, but to concentrate on my business, I quit that job and dropped out of college. I had to trust my instincts and follow my heart. I would figure it out as I went along.

## Magical Blooms

I started Magical Blooms with only $500 to my name. I spent $100 on a business license, $100 on business cards, and $100 on flowers—and with the $100 I had left, I bought a couple of outfits. I started to run the business out of my garage.

Every morning, I would wake up at 4 a.m. and drive an hour to downtown Los Angeles and buy flowers wholesale. My store was open 8 a.m. to 8 p.m., Monday through Friday, and weekends 9 a.m. to 5 p.m. I worked a lot, but I was willing to give it my all. I was never shown how to hire and train employees, so I learned in real time. I dealt with no-shows and some who stole from the shop, but I also had employees who have stayed in my life to this day and whom I love so very much. I was a novice and didn't understand profit

margins. If a customer wanted a $50 arrangement, at first I would spend $50 on the flowers—hence, no profit. I loved designing flowers so much that it felt like I was stealing someone's money if I charged them more than what I paid for the blooms. I knocked on the doors of Los Angeles shops to introduce myself and to offer to design their flower arrangements. I slowly built up my clientele and landed some bigger accounts, including yacht parties, hotels, and weddings. I learned about profit and running a business.

I quickly outgrew my garage, and my landlord told me that I had to find a storefront to continue my business. Soon after, I found a retail store for rent. Although I didn't love the space, the owner of the building trusted me and was willing to hand over the keys. There was one hitch, though: I didn't have enough money for the deposit. I was lucky enough to be working with a generous woman who had faith in me. She was getting married soon, loved my work, and wanted me to arrange the flowers for her wedding. In exchange, she wrote me a check for the deposit. I moved out of my apartment and moved in with my aunt Wendy so that I could afford the rent for the store. My aunt had been a constant in my life—I spent time with her at my grandparents' house, and she was a support system throughout my childhood. She never had kids, so she became like a second mom to me. I also sold my car and used the delivery van as my main mode of transportation.

When I opened the doors to the first Magical Blooms store in Hermosa Beach, my vision was to create a true home away from home for my customers, just as I had experienced in the

FLOWER℞

**"I'm here for you."**
*Snapdragons, roses, misty blue, dahlias. Budget: Stick to what you can afford—it's the gesture that counts.*

first flower shop where I worked. Eventually, I moved to my current location in Redondo Beach, but my original goal has not changed: to offer a welcoming space for my community. I have now been in this location for more than twenty years. When customers walk into the store, I want the shop to feel like a warm hug. In fact, during those first years in business, I would give every person who walked into my shop an actual hug. I'm all about energy. I'm all about vibes.

At Magical Blooms, I always have music pumping and cool containers for flowers—whether it's made of opaque ceramic so you can't see the water or has an inspiring shape or a fun texture or finish. I reach for fun, creative containers I can pull off the shelves, so no two arrangements look alike. My philosophy is that the container should not compete with the flowers. It's more important for the vase to complement the arrangement so you can appreciate the beauty of the flowers. My clients trust me to create designs that may be a little wild—I love using surprising pops of colors and textures—but at the end of the day, it's the flower energy that leads the way. Anyone can put a bunch of flowers together, but I pour in the prayer of the design.

In my early years, every dollar I made I put back into the business to improve the shop and to offer better-quality flowers. Do you know what it is like to walk into a cooler and see so much beauty? All I wanted to do was to buy

beautiful flowers and fill my store with them. I took out no loans and used only the money I earned. I did this alone with no family helping me financially. I showed up every day and never gave up. I was *not* a numbers girl: I avoided accounting. Looking at numbers gave me anxiety. I just wanted to work and show up and play. The idea of a budget was nonexistent. And yet, I remember when I had my first year of selling $20,000 worth of flowers and earning $500,000.

I'm a funky designer who adds a little bit of magic—a secret sauce that you don't even know is missing—to each flower design. When I'm arranging a design, I feel like a kid in a candy shop. I go into an altered state and let my instincts do the work, selecting stems and blooms that surprise and delight. A Magical Blooms Designer's Choice might include a mixture of sweet peas, fiddle fern, kangaroo paws, cockscomb, rosemary, and mint. These are combinations you don't often find in other flower shops.

For the last five years, I've worked with only high-quality farm-grown flowers, so my flowers are on a different frequency and of a higher caliber than what most shops offer. As you will come to learn in this book, buying flowers from the grocery store is a huge no-no. Just as Anthony Bourdain unveiled the truth about the restaurant industry, I will let you in on the insider secrets that retail stores selling flowers don't want you to know. It will change the way you think about and buy flowers.

Another thing that sets Magical Blooms apart is that we always make our arrangements fresh and on the fly. People who walk into a typical flower shop admire coolers full of premade designs at predetermined prices; everyone is in a hurry and doesn't have time to wait. We never make arrangements in advance, hoping to sell them off the shelf. I understand the emotional connection to flowers and the transformative stories told through them, which is why I never design an arrangement without knowing the intention or emotional state of the client. Whether the occasion is a romantic connection or heartbreak, death or celebration, we rely on flowers to emotionally connect our soul to our surroundings. Rather than calling or texting a friend or loved one and saying "I'm sorry for your loss," we send flowers as a gesture to acknowledge their emotional state. When they look at the flowers sitting on the counter, they will know they are supported. Flowers provide an energy that lasts. Behind every flower grown, arranged, and given, there's a story that tells the journey of where the flower goes and how it helps someone's life, relationship, or connection.

## Connecting with Flowers on Another Frequency

I didn't have much of a relationship with my dad when I was growing up. I would see him about once a year. It wasn't until the tail end of my father's life, when he was dying, that I understood my connection to him and the origins of my spirituality and sixth sense.

When my dad was in hospice, I started receiving calls from famous psychics, asking, "How is your father?" I was so confused. Who were these people and how did they know that my dad was sick? He didn't have a cell phone or a computer—he had no connection to the outside world at this point. I asked my dad what the heck was going on. This is when he told me that he was a clairvoyant. People called him the Wizard. He had made connections with all of these clairvoyants who now somehow knew he was on his way out of the physical world and that he had a message for me. This is when my dad told me that I possessed the same superpower. He said, "Ask the universe, daughter, and get out of your own way."

FLOWERx

**Strong flowers for a lasting friendship.**
*Pincushion flowers, wax flowers, proteas.*

From that point on, I put his words into action. If I needed a new client or to manifest money, all I needed to do was ask the universe and get out of my own way, and it would happen. After my dad died, just before the COVID-19 pandemic, the flowers started to talk to me on a different level. Their messages were coming in clearly and strongly, to the point where I often said out loud what I was hearing. I started sharing the flowers' messages with others because the frequency was so intense. I have since learned how to use this magic for the benefit of others.

For years I was buying cut flowers from wholesalers but had never experienced the blooms in their pure and natural environment, untouched and not yet cut from the ground. It wasn't until my first trip to a flower farm, experiencing flowers from the root—and seeing hundreds of thousands of them growing together—that my relationship with flowers changed forever, becoming otherworldly. The flowers were almost like a symphony, all in harmony, singing a beautiful song that only I could hear.

When everything shut down during the pandemic, most florists were forced to close their shops, but something in me told me not to follow suit, that I was an essential business. I joined an organization called CalFlowers, which granted me direct access to flower farms. I started calling local growers to let them know that I wanted to work with them directly. At that time, flower farms had no choice but to discard fully matured flowers instead of selling them. There was a sliver of opportunity for me to get in my car with my son, Jack, who was nine years old at the time, and visit these farms. We drove to the Resendiz Brothers Farm in Rainbow Valley several times, which is about two hours away, as well as other farms—some were as far as a six-hour drive from our home. I was appreciating the flowers and getting to know the local growers through their stories of their own personal experiences with starting their flower farms.

I remember how excited I was when I pulled up to the first farm, in Rainbow Valley. On our way down to the farm I asked Jack what he missed most about school being closed. "Mom, I'm really going to miss out on the field trips," he replied. I told him, "Jack, you're about to go on the best field trips of your life." When we arrived in Rainbow Valley, it felt like we took a trip to Hawaii. The farm grew incredible proteas, pincushions, leucadendrons, leucodermas, and wax flowers. It was the most spectacular day. The sun was shining, yet there was a mist, and all the flowers were glowing.

The first time I walked up to a pincushion bush, the flowers started to talk to me. I touched them and felt their energy. A pincushion resembles, as you can imagine, a real pincushion—the flower has one spike, and it shoots out a bunch of pins. When it's tight, this flower is structured and organized, but when it shoots out, it creates exuberant energy. Pincushions usually come in shades of orange or yellow. Sometimes you even see double heads. This flower is incredibly tough—it can withstand a lot and is even drought resistant. However, it has a very fragile head, so if you tap on it, the head could easily break. The message

FLOWER$_{x}$

**Clearing loneliness.** *Pincushion flowers.*

that the pincushions offered me that day was "I am here for you." When I touched them, the energy was transcendent.

Pincushions remain my support system. It's the same feeling I experienced as a little girl when I spent time with my grandpa's roses. I often tell my clients that if you're run down and need a fierce jolt of energy, you want to have pincushion flowers near you at all times, especially when you're trying to make bold moves and you need that little extra punch. Being near pincushions is almost like drinking caffeine.

The power each flower shares with me is not a meaning you will find in a Google search. These messages have to do with spirituality and often have specific significance for me or my customer.

## What Is a Flower Prescription?

I have a belief system that works with nature. Flowers talk to me, and I listen. I prescribe flowers as a way of healing. A flower prescription is my version of a flower arrangement. Each flower has a meaning, and each design has a meaning. I pull the energies of the flowers, tell the customer which flowers hold specific meanings for them, and write down their personal flower prescription. It's really about clearing energy and bringing forward what the customer is worthy of and what they deserve. Flowers can help with anxiety, depression, and loneliness—they are like antidepressants. But they are also a reminder that we can quickly change the energy of a room with a gorgeous arrangement of flowers.

In 2013, I earned my master's degree in spiritual psychology because I wanted to gain a stronger theoretical and practical foundation for my work. Over the years, my flower prescriptions have evolved from something casual to more of a clinical practice. Customers can book an appointment with me to talk about flowers—I call these "flower sessions." I set aside time for them, and just like going to a therapist, it's a one-on-one hour-long session in my back office. I work with many clients on a regular basis, and sometimes people come into the shop and I have time available and can do a quick intuitive reading and share a flower message. I always want to be present and of service so customers can connect to me in the moment.

A flower prescription session can best be described as a hybrid therapy / life coaching / psychic session. It can be unnerving for my clients, but it also opens them in a way that they have never experienced before. Clients have no idea what's in store for them when they walk in the door. They walk away from their sessions

FLOWER$_x$

**Mental wellness.** *Sunflowers, roses, dahlias, rosemary, kiwi vine, marigolds.*

with a feeling of wonderment and a newfound sense of purpose.

I start my sessions with a series of questions in order to understand each client's story. Who are the flowers for? What is the occasion? I explain that one size doesn't fit all. For example, I would never prescribe the same arrangement for a celebration as I would for someone experiencing grief. The energy is completely different, and the flowers need to reflect that energy.

At Magical Blooms, we offer multiple ways for people to experience their flower prescription. The more traditional option is to allow me or one of our florists to create a custom arrangement, but customers can also book a table to create their own arrangements, take a flower class, or even receive a flower box shipped to their home. If they choose to do their own flower arranging with flowers I have prescribed to them, there's music playing in the background and they're able to touch the flowers and feel the emotion and the excitement. They can take a break from their day to just play. It's like a high; when they are touching and feeling flowers, their senses are flaring off like fireworks. At the end of the process, they feel so accomplished and proud that they have designed something beautiful to display.

**Clear communication.**
*White hydrangeas.*

## The Healing Power of Flowers

I've learned that connecting to Mother Nature clears the mind. We often have the answers to our problems within us. I know that the energies of certain flowers can help us access those answers. When you place these flowers in front of you and take the time to connect with them by touching, feeling, and breathing them in, those answers will emerge.

Flowers can act like medication and provide a visual aid around your house to remind you of their energies. For example, if I'm having a hard time communicating, I place hydrangeas on my kitchen counter or by my keyboard. Instead of wanting to scream or yell out of frustration, I'll look at the flower and allow its energies to help me communicate in a calmer state. Using flowers is a new form of therapy, and I believe I am the only flower doctor around. I've never met another florist who does what I do.

Flowers are considered a luxury. They are the last item to be purchased when we're in an economic crisis. When gas is overpriced, inflation rises, and rents hit an all-time high,

FLOWERx

**Speak more softly.**
*Pink hydrangeas.*

FLOWER℞

**Get well.** *Sunflowers, acacia, snapdragons, chamomile.*

flowers are almost always cut from household budgets, unless it's for a very special occasion. This should not be the case. Flowers are an essential form of self-care, and they don't need to be expensive to be powerful, either. Flowers should be a nonnegotiable part of home decor—like apples or bananas in a kitchen. They make the house more inviting, and they make you feel more beautiful. They also make guests who visit your home feel more welcome.

As you will discover in this book, we all have the potential to allow flowers to work their magic in our lives. I encourage you to look at flowers differently after reading this book and hearing the stories of how flowers have helped so many people live healthier and happier lives. Flowers have a short life, which reminds us that *we* have a short life, too, and we have to make good choices.

FLOWER℞

**"It's time!"** *Proteas, viburnum berry, hanging amaranthus, Mokara orchids, poppy pods, umbrella ferns, monstera leaves, grevilleas.*

CHAPTER 1

# celebrations: cheers to life!

There are two ways to think about times of celebrations: The first is focused on you, the one who is being celebrated, and the second is to share in the joy of another. When you've accomplished something and want to revel in the moment, the flowers perform a different duty. While a time of celebration can be fun, there are often feelings of anxiousness, too. In the time leading up to that celebration, there was likely a lot of planning involved, which can cast a shadow on the present moment. The core value of flowers is to keep you calm and help you absorb and enjoy the celebration that you have worked so hard to create. These flowers will anchor you in the present and help you honor and appreciate your achievements—whether it's a new job, new house, new marriage, new baby, new year, or new chapter in your life. Now you can enjoy it by opening your eyes and seeing all that love around you.

When it's time to celebrate others, there is nothing quite like a gorgeous bouquet of buds to lift the spirits and amplify a special occasion. I like to think of giving flowers as "parallel energy," meaning that the flowers you are giving someone to commemorate an occasion should reflect the energy and joy of that moment. In other words, flowers should match the theme of the event. Rather than giving a random assortment of flowers or asking the florist to choose for you, this chapter will help guide your flower selection so you can bring even more joy and love to those happy moments in life.

## Mama Power

A customer named Javier came into the shop recently looking really nervous. I asked him what I could do to help. He hesitated and got choked up. He told me that his girlfriend just found out that she was pregnant and was an emotional wreck. I knew I had to design him something unforgettable. I started with oregano and told him to rub the oregano between his fingers and smell the scent. It acts as a slow vital medicine that says, “I’m here for you, I am not giving up on you, and you’re going to be okay.” Rubbing and pinching the oregano activates its fragrance. Touching and interacting with the flowers in this way may be an unusual concept to most people, but when my sixth sense kicks in, the directions I give to my clients can seem to be out of the ordinary. I encourage all my customers to touch their arrangements to activate their senses and get the full essence of the flowers. I have drawn this from my own intuition and what has worked for me. It’s a quiet but effective way to keep the nervous system calm and remove negative thoughts.

Then I added mint to the arrangement, which represents a soothing tonic—we drink mint tea to soothe our bellies after a meal. As we smell mint, it also stimulates our brain and acts as a calming reset. When I put the arrangement together and the flowers in the vase, I told him to smell the flowers and herbs. He looked at me and smiled. Then I added beautiful little buttermilk flowers along with some red roses so he could show his girlfriend that he was in it for the long haul. I softened it with a pink rose and a purple or white flower called misty blue, to fill in the spaces around the primary flower arrangement.

I wanted to pump up her energy, so I added rice flowers (above), which smell a bit like marijuana. They are a lovely accent flower and an interesting texture to add to an arrangement. Whenever I want to ramp up the energy in a design, I add rice flowers—sometimes last minute—to give it dimension and activate the frequency of the flower.

I told Javier to give his girlfriend the design but not tell her what I said and just listen to her and be there for her. I knew she was probably feeling completely out of alignment and that bringing her those flowers would be the best medicine.

## IT'S A . . . BABY! MILKWEED: THE SECRET KEEPERS

I call this the butterfly flower because they attract loads of caterpillars who cocoon and later develop into their secret identity—butterflies. When you are trying to harvest a new idea but want to keep it private or you're having a hard time keeping a secret, th s is your flower. Buttermilk flowers have a delicate energy. They come in yellow, orange, and red tones, and they are a late spring and summer flower but sometimes you can still enjoy them in the fall. Nothing is more exciting than sharing your news, but waiting is the hardest part. When you need to hold on to a secret—like a pregnancy or plans to move—buttermilk will help you keep silent for a moment. When the stem is cut, a milky liquid releases. I suggest using an opaque container and avoiding a clear vase unless you plan to change your water daily.

When you're celebrating a baby's birth, I suggest sending roses and hydrangeas. Roses represent the heart chakra, and hydrangeas are a communication flower, so when you combine the two, it's a story of love, harmony, support, and communication. Conveniently, these flowers are accessible all year round. Forgo traditional rules of sending shades of blue for a boy or pink for a girl—the idea of creating a flower arrangement to "match" the gender of the baby is dated and not what we're about at Magical Blooms. We thankfully live in a world that is accepting of the many views on gender, and I love to celebrate that by sending new parents flowers in any color under the rainbow. Yellow and white together are classic and beautiful for welcoming a new baby.

New parents are often overwhelmed. My number one rule when sending flowers to new parents is to not send them to the hospital; instead, send them to their home. As lovely as it is to receive flowers at the hospital, many new parents leave the hospital within two days, and the flowers will be appreciated so much more at home. When they're alone at night feeding the baby, seeing the flowers will remind them of your love and support.

### FLOWERS AND PETS

Many flowers are potentially toxic to pets. I always recommend that my clients consult online resources, such as the ASPCA website, in case there are periodic updates. It's best practice for those with pets to place the arrangement out of reach of animals and to avoid any tall arrangements that could potentially get knocked over by your furry friends.

## Know Your Audience

I love it when a customer comes in who knows exactly what they want—or in one particular case, a man who knew precisely what types of flowers his wife loves. I was designing at my desk when Jake, a hip young father who's a regular customer, came in. He had just snuck away from his job and wanted an adorable bouquet with vibrant pink peonies, fuchsia, Singapore orchids, hellebores, mint, and red roses wrapped in butcher paper with a white and a pink bow. He said it was his three-year-old daughter's birthday, and he wanted to give the bouquet to her mom, his wife. I thought it was so sweet! It's so important to acknowledge the mom on a child's birthday. A man taking time aside to buy flowers for his wife on their daughter's birthday is so special. What made this extra special is that the man took extra time to remember the specific blooms his wife loves. That goes a long way when giving flowers, trust me.

## Birthday Flowers

For birthdays, flowers could be monochromatic in the birthday recipient's favorite color. For example, I love yellow, so I would love to receive flowers in all shades of yellow, from pale to bright. It's also fun to give vibrant, colorful flowers of many shades for a birthday. People don't often buy colorful flowers for themselves—so for someone's birthday it's nice to celebrate them with hot pinks, bright blues, neon yellows, and bold oranges in seasonal flowers.

FLOWER$_x$

**Celebration.** *Pink and yellow roses, yarrow, mini carnations, mint, rosemary, oregano, orlaya.*

FLOWERx

**House party or casual barbecue.** *Yarrow, chamomile, acacia, bird's nest, black-eyed Susan.*

## SMILAX

Smilax is one of my favorite lengthy greeneries to use when decorating chandeliers and is perfect for taller designs that require draped greenery because it's light, fluffy, and super dramatic. It is playful in sweetheart table arrangements at weddings, staircase décor, or fireplaces. I used to hesitate to use it because when I would order it from wholesalers, it would look old. But when I went to the farm and experienced it in living color, I was in awe of its rows, strands, and thickness. I felt like I had walked into a divine space. When you're having a party at your house and want to make it feel festive, the last place you think of decorating with greenery is your lighting. Get a bag of smilax and play with it! Display it on your fixtures—they will look angelic. Place it on your stairway—it will look heavenly. Surround a birthday cake with it, and just like that, you can make it come alive.

## Creative Endeavors

A client recently called the shop wanting to send flowers to their friend, a playwright whose play was debuting on stage in New York City. She wanted to know what type of flowers to send to congratulate her on this creative endeavor. This type of celebration is a bit different from a bridal party or a job promotion. In this case, the client was flying into New York for the debut. I recommended that she find a local florist—either with help from the hotel concierge or Google—and make a phone call to the shop to have a conversation with them about the arrangement as opposed to just placing an order online.

Any experienced florist will be over the moon to provide flowers for such an exciting occasion, and if they don't sound excited, move on to another shop. For this type of occasion, ask the florist for a "designer's choice presentation wrap bouquet," which is flat on one side and bountiful and fluffy on the other side, so the recipient can easily hold it after the performance, and it won't lay awkwardly in her hands at the theater. Tell the florist your friend's favorite colors, ask them to use flowers that are in season, and request that they put a nice big bow around it. When in doubt, you can always send a dozen red roses, wrapped. Most importantly, ask the florist to use a water wrap or water picks so the flowers stay fresh.

FLOWER℞

**Total love and commitment.** *Red roses, trailing jasmine, mint, oregano.*

## Anniversary

One of the sweetest gestures is bringing your partner a bouquet designed with the same flowers they held when they walked down the aisle. This is a romantic way to remember your wedding day. The card message will set the tone. In the card, reminisce about a special moment from your wedding or write some of the lyrics of your wedding song. If you're planning a getaway to celebrate your anniversary, it does not mean you should skip out on flowers. You can order flowers and arrange with the hotel to have them sent to the room—there's nothing better than the surprise of walking into the hotel room and seeing flowers waiting for you.

## Bridal Wishes

You just got engaged, and you want to ask your best friend to be in your wedding party. There is no better way than to send them a flower bouquet with a note to say how honored you would be to have them by your side at your wedding. I love sunflowers for this, to help bring in rays of sunshine; add white roses for that bridal feeling and greenery—a simple design in a container.

Sunflowers are innocent flowers that represent joyful moments, and yellow represents friendship. When you're asking your friend to be a part of your wedding, you are asking them to support you during this incredible journey of getting married. On the flip side, if your best friend just got engaged, you want to express your love and support. Send a bouquet—sunflowers are also perfect for this. If your friend favors a clean, modern, and sleek aesthetic, a pure white arrangement with white hydrangeas and white roses is simply beautiful!

## GARDENIAS

Gardenias are delicate and beautifully fragrant, yet super fragile. Their simple elegance shines whether placed in a small bud vase, floating in water, or worn as a corsage. They are a lovely gesture for moms or grandmothers on Mother's Day or birthdays, especially if you're heading to brunch. However, these beauties bruise and wilt quickly once cut from the stem, so it's best to keep them refrigerated until it's time to use them. Despite their fragility, they're stunning in bridal bouquets or even tucked into your hair for a special occasion, bringing a timeless and romantic charm wherever they go.

## Fri-Yay!

One of my favorite things is to give flowers on a Friday. We work so hard Monday through Thursday that when Friday comes you get to kick it, relax, and enjoy. Flowers set the tone for a great weekend, and you can really enjoy them if you're home much of the weekend—you wake up slower, sip your coffee slower, make your breakfast, and gaze over and look at those flowers. During the week you're in and out of the house, running around to work, school drop-off, and errands, so you can't enjoy them as much.

I love using flowers to set my intention for the weekend. If I have red roses sitting on the counter on Friday, I am purposefully setting the tone for a romantic weekend. If it's a colorful bouquet of mixed seasonal flowers, it is foreshadowing a happy weekend filled with playfulness. When I want to feel more Zen and relaxed, I love to give myself a yellow color palette in flowers—roses, marigolds, billy balls, alstroemeria, mums, sunflowers, and loose greenery. Let this become a lifestyle: Pick up flowers on Fridays, no matter what.

FLOWERx

**Congratulations.**
*Sunflowers, marigolds, billy balls, alstroemeria, chrysanthemums, greenery.*

## New Home

Your friend moved into a new place, and they're having a housewarming party. Or a new neighbor just moved in next door. What do you do? It doesn't matter if it's a small apartment or a large home, what's most important is welcoming your friend to their new domain. You will want to wait at least a couple weeks after they move in to send the flowers. This way, your friend will be unpacked and can actually admire the flowers in their newly settled space.

Do you know the style of the house? Is it Cape Cod, Italian, sleek and modern, or rustic cabin vibes? Sharing this info with the florist gives them creative freedom to design something that complements the home, working within your budget and what's in season. When the arrangement matches the style of the house, it becomes more than just flowers—it becomes part of their space.

If you don't know the style of their house, use their personality type to help guide you. Are they professionals or artistic types? Reserved or free spirits? If they are sophisticated, go with something white and modern. If they are more of a hippie or wild child, send something more vibrant. Consider hydrangeas, roses, and perhaps some ranunculus with a little bit of lush greenery—ideally, seasonal flowers in a muted tone. I would prescribe a nice white ceramic container in any case—it's more stylish and current than a glass vase—and stick with what's in season. You don't want something too big or overpowering, especially if you don't know the size of the home.

Anyone can stop by the grocery store and pick up an orchid, but that's boring! Talk to your florist and guide them in creating something special.

## TUBEROSE

If someone calls the flower shop asking for a fragrant design, tuberoses are my go-to stem. While they may not be the flashiest flowers, their scent is like pure heaven—filling any space with an intoxicating, sweet perfume that lingers for about a week. Tuberose invites you to slow down, speak softer, listen more, and respond less. Let their fragrance remind you to breathe in love and add calmness to your life—reducing stress with each inhale. They're a wonderful gift for housewarmings in particular, but are also great for birthdays, anniversaries, or wishing someone well. Almost everyone falls in love with the fragrance of tuberose.

FLOWERx

**Freedom.** *Lavender, yellow roses, misty blue, rosemary, asters, oregano.*

## Work Anniversary, Promotion, or New Job

Sending a beautiful arrangement to a friend, family member, or loved one for their work achievement can surprise and delight the recipient. Consider a smaller footprint so it won't overwhelm their desk. I love using colors like purple and yellow—roses, spray roses, misty blue as a filler, and a sprig of herbs, like oregano or rosemary, in a white container. I would also advise using sunflowers, snapdragons, and chamomile. This bouquet should be subtle, not intense—it's intended to be a visual aid to soothe their nerves after putting forth so much effort to achieve their goal. They will be able to retain the joyful memory of those flowers sitting on their desk long after they are gone, and their brain will also remember how the flowers calmed them. Celebratory flowers for a work achievement offer extended acknowledgment of hard work—almost like a continuous round of applause.

For a work promotion, I suggest yellow sunflowers, yellow roses, white lisianthus, and greenery—these are bright and fun colors mixed with a calming element. Adding white into the design can also be fabulous. If the florist doesn't have those exact flowers, it's okay; just tell them the color palette and work with what is in season.

## KANGAROO PAWS: MANIFEST

I am the queen of manifesting things in my life. I ask the universe for what I want and then get out of my own way. Kangaroo paws are the ultimate manifesting flower. They are anchored in the ground and sprout up super quick, as if the universe itself manifested them and they just magically appeared. The stems are notoriously difficult to cut, so extracting them from the ground is almost impossible. They come in all sorts of fun colors. These unique flowers are super long-lasting and have taller stems with a furry texture—they literally look like a paw. Be careful what you put out into the universe. Be mindful and focus on what it is that you really want. If it's finding a new job, home, or partner in life—or even just walking into a store and finding the right dress to wear—you must visualize, feel, and believe that it's coming to you. When it is supposed to show up, it will. The faster you let go after declaring what it is you want, the faster the universe will listen to you.

## Graduation

If you're celebrating a school graduation, you can never go wrong with yellow and white flowers: sunflowers, yellow roses, snapdragons, and some greenery with a little lavender to calm the graduate's nervous system. Yellow and white represent happiness and new beginnings. For high school or college graduations, you don't need to spend a lot of money. The flowers may not last as long, especially if the graduate is party hopping for days and may forget to refill the water. For a fun and wearable way to celebrate your graduate, try asking a florist if they can make a flower crown or a lei and to include flowers in the colors of the graduate's school. Make sure to call the florist at least one week in advance to place the order. If you show up on the day of the graduation, your lei will be made up of leftovers.

If you're going out to eat after the graduation ceremony, find a nearby florist and order flowers to be delivered to the restaurant. You want to add some life to the table on this joyous occasion. If you're coming in from out of town, ask the restaurant for their recommendation for a nearby florist. Tell the florist you want a low-profile arrangement (you want to be able to see and talk to the person sitting across from you) and have the flowers delivered about an hour before your reservation. The flowers will set the tone for beauty, excitement, celebration, and support.

## Magical Blooms Story

One day at the shop I received a call from a woman who was helping her friend's husband purchase flowers for her birthday. He was deployed out of the country, but he wanted to send beautiful flowers to his wife on her special day. One of the most generous things you can do for a friend is help their significant other with flower-buying for a birthday, anniversary, or other special occasion. Whether they're deployed overseas or just at a loss about where to start, as their friend, you can be a huge help.

## Thank You for Celebrating Me

If your friend is throwing you a birthday party or a baby shower, always send them flowers the day before the celebration with a note of gratitude. It's especially thoughtful for your friend to receive the flowers *before* the party so they have extra flowers for the event. If you forget to send them before the party, though, make sure to send flowers the day after the party. Your friend took time out of their life to host your loved ones, and sending a thank-you with a lovely bouquet is a meaningful way to express deep appreciation.

**Congratulations on pregnancy.** *Garden roses in pink and purple tones, cremon mums, stock, trailing jasmine, rosemary, veronica, sweet peas, lisianthus, lavender.*

## Wedding Countdown

When you're planning a wedding, there's a great deal of stress, and it's nice and thoughtful to show your support by sending a small bouquet to your future spouse every month leading up the wedding date. I suggest you send it along with a little note to remind them of the real reason why you're going through all this planning and stress—and that you're so excited to get married. Surprise them with the arrangement and move it around the house—one day it could be on the kitchen counter; another day it could be at the front entrance or next to the bedside. In the note, include how many more days are left before you say "I do." After you get married, carry on this tradition by sending a striking bouquet once every season.

## Wedding Prescription

You can never go wrong with a timeless palette of white and green flowers—classic, elegant, and always in season. Don't feel pressured to match the wedding colors; instead, opt for what's blooming naturally. Hydrangeas, roses, lisianthus, dusty miller, alstroemeria, tulips, rosemary, sweet pea, peonies, and white lilacs create a soft, serene vibe. And yes, a hint of blush or faint pink is perfectly fine—it's sweet and soothing, helping to calm nerves while maintaining that effortless romantic charm.

## Happy House Anniversary

It's the anniversary of owning your house—why not celebrate with flowers? Place a bouquet in the kitchen and celebrate. You put in a lot of energy and effort to get to homeownership—not to mention the decorating or perhaps the remodeling of the home. Celebrate your one-year anniversary saying, "Yay, we did it!"

## GERBERA DAISIES: GET HAPPY

Gerbera daisies are the happiest flowers on the planet. If you're feeling down, go buy yourself colorful gerbera daisies and place them everywhere in your home or office. Take more walks, go out and get fresh air. If you had a conversation with someone having a tough time, this is truly the best pick-me-up flower, whether it's a single stem or bunch of ten stems. Place them in a vase—no other flowers necessary. Do a test when you're at the store: See what color makes you smile and pick that color. Here are some tips for colors: red for countering heartbreak; yellow for wellness; orange for overcoming self-doubt; pink to help cleanse yourself of unhealthy friendships; white for soothing grief; two-toned for dealing with the loss of a job or a home.

## WHEN YOU'RE THE HOST

When you're having a party, it's important to understand where to place flowers in your home. Always have an arrangement on the dining room table. Avoid anything too tall or grand—choose low arrangements so people can have conversations over the flowers. If you have a bar, place flowers on the right side of the bar so it looks pretty and festive. A small arrangement in the restroom, such as a cute bud vase with flowers, is a mood booster. Focus on the areas where your guests will be spending time. For outdoor gatherings, colorful plants always add a touch of warmth and fun.

## THISTLE

Thistle may look like a scrappy roadside weed, but today it's one of the trendiest flowers to style with, especially for beach or desert weddings and events. Its rugged, spiky texture adds an unexpected edge to any arrangement, and it's perfect for mixing in a bud vase to complement other blooms with a touch of unique flair. Beyond its cool looks, thistle is like a guardian for your energy—it helps you stay grounded, make smart choices, and avoid bad decisions. If something feels off or like it could cause trouble, you're probably right. Let thistle remind you to steer clear of conflict and potential issues and stay on the path of good choices and positive vibes.

CHAPTER 2

# success at school and work

## Meeting Deadlines and Mastering Time Management

Life can be frantic. If we're not good at organizing our time, it can lead to system overload. To help master the art of time management, one of my favorite greeneries is mint. For years, I shied away from working with mint because I thought it would die quickly; however, when you buy it from the farm, it is actually a long-lasting stem. When mint is cared for properly, it can last up to three weeks.

As soon as the mint arrives, cut and cool the stems in water or a cooler to bring them to life after they've traveled from the farm. Their essence reels in frantic energy. Once you smell the mint, your brain receives an immediate burst of *Ahh, that's nice*. But the feeling goes much deeper than just the smell. What I love most about mint is the texture. The leaves have a three-dimensional, lizard-like feel, and when you touch them with your fingers, it zaps the brain with energy. The vibrancy of the bright green gives you a facelift, meaning that when you look at mint, your face will glow, your eyes will expand, and your lips will smile. When mint connects your brain to your heart, you feel instant relief. I suggest placing the mint in front of you—at your desk or wherever you work. Don't just cut it and put it in a vase. Put your hands on the mint, rub it, and feel the texture of the leaves in order to connect with the part of your brain that helps you feel good.

## Focus

The number one flower for focus is the chrysanthemum. It's long-lasting and powerful, with petals that act like cheerleaders. It has a powerful scent to help awaken the senses. Chrysanthemums are hard to destroy and can last up to a month. Their energy is powerful—the chrysanthemums are telling you that they're rooting for you to stay clear and focus on the next task.

## Motivation and Discipline

It's normal to lose that initial passion you harnessed after starting a new project or a new job. That first spark of excitement eventually becomes more ordinary. The flowers I prescribe to flood energy, motivation, and discipline will give you a charge and help keep you focused. You will want a combination of pincushions and a type of flower called billy ball. This flower is yellow, so consider adding blue thistle flowers to the arrangement. I like this combination because it will give you a charge. When you run out of battery and feel like you need that extra bit of motivation and discipline, these flowers will help get you back on track.

## Studying and School Stress

The pressures of school are a familiar feeling regardless of your age. Meeting deadlines and getting good grades are always top of mind for students. I like to look at it differently. What if we can change our attitude and discover that we love learning a certain subject and nurture

FLOWERx

**A lasting statement of power and independence.** *Protea, billy balls, Alpine sea holly.*

**ABOVE, CLOCKWISE FROM TOP LEFT:** Marigolds, billy balls, black-eyed Susan.

that subject with the help of flowers? To help ease school-related anxiety and to aid with studying, find flowers in shades of yellow, white, and orange. To warm your environment and to destress, I suggest setting flowers, such as marigolds, by your computer or school papers. If you have a test, make sure to have orange flowers; orange screams, "I'm supporting you!"

Certain flowers have a more powerful voice when combined. I love bringing together orange spray roses, billy balls, mums, sunflowers, marigolds, and snapdragons to help neutralize

the stress of school. When you're in school, there is so much pressure. It can feel so serious. To help lighten the load, I love this combination. It helps foster a sense of support and playfulness. Orange spray flowers offer supportive love; billy balls are super friendly and playful, but they're also strong-minded flowers. When you combine these with mums, which are also supportive flowers, and sunflowers, they will lower your stress levels. Marigolds are spiritual flowers that help you connect with a higher power, and snapdragons are your cheerleaders. Together they release a happy vibration that will bring an instant smile to your face. You'll feel like someone's high-fiving you.

## Getting That Promotion

Let's say you know you've been a rockstar performer at work and you're hoping for a promotion. You're killing it in sales, you're showing up on time and achieving all your goals, and now you're ready to take that next step. To demonstrate your power, you will need a vibrant flower.

If you want to take charge of getting that promotion, I recommend a combo act: The first flower is bird of paradise—an indestructible flower. It can withstand any storm. It is even hard to cut! The other flower is bougainvillea—it has thorns to keep predators away, but it's also vibrant. Bougainvillea are perennials and will grow back in your garden each year.

You might notice a cloud of bougainvillea cascading over an arch, proving that it can spring to life anywhere.

The reason why you will get a promotion is because you're eye-catching, you're achieving something important, and you're vibrant and unstoppable—just like bougainvillea.

## Students Struggling at School

Parents know the amount of stress their kid feels when struggling to live up to expectations. Helping your child meet their homework deadlines requires commitment. Carnations can help. They are available all year round in many sizes and come in white, red, pink, and fuchsia. We want carnations around us because of their consistency and stability. They are nearly indestructible, too. Just try to remove a singular petal from the carnation—you can't! All the petals must be pulled out together. It's similar to the attitude you want to impart to your child: You need to go all-in to achieve your goals.

## Flowers to Send to a Client or Referrer

Whether you work for yourself or for a company, sending flowers as a thank-you to a client, business associate, or a referrer signifies that you are a class act. Depending on the season, I'd suggest a medium-sized arrangement in white and yellow, with shades of pink.

## Career Decision Breakthrough

If you're considering a career move, starting a business, or some other big work-related change, remember to take the time you need, to peel back the layers and ultimately find your true goal.

To help my clients find clarity and make decisions organically and playfully, I created the following six-week process involving a different flower each week. Try it yourself: Each flower has its own message for you, and your interactions with them can help you work through the decision-making process. You already have the answer within you.

## WEEK 1: Orange Roses

Orange roses will encourage someone to make new commitments. Place at least a dozen in the kitchen and a minimum of three roses in the office. No greenery or other filler flowers are needed—stick to strictly orange roses during this time. Smile and look at the roses, repeating a positive statement as many times as possible, connecting to them for one full week and being open to new opportunities.

## WEEK 2: White Stock

Whites, yellows, shades of pinks, purples, and peaches—you will love stock once you smell it. However, that lovely fragrance has a time limit. When you first get stock, it smells delicious, but after about five to seven days, it should be thrown away because its odor turns foul. This is a great flower to add into a design with other flowers. Tall and fluffy, this bloom reminds us that we need to be more kind to ourselves. When we are kind to ourselves, we can receive kindness from others. Being hard on yourself is not healthy. You cannot control how others are going to behave around you, but you *can* control how you respond or limit your time with them.

## WEEK 3: Lilies

This week is all about lilies, specifically the Stargazer lily or Casablanca lily. The focus this week is on forgiveness. Place these flowers where there's the most activity or where you'll see them the most, such as on the kitchen countertop. The energy of the lilies is all about trusting and forgiving yourself. Some emotions might surface—you might cry or feel angry, disappointed, or even jealous of others who have already started their own businesses. The goal this week is to feel all the emotions.

## WEEK 4: Cosmos

Any color of cosmos will work, but multicolor are my preference: white, pink, or lavender. The intention of cosmos is for you to learn to stand up for yourself. The flowers should be placed in an area of the house where you spend most of your time.

## WEEK 5: Pincushions

The focus this week is on ushering in excitement and happiness. Pincushion flowers should be placed by the bedside and in as many areas around the house as possible. Put on inspiring music and touch the pincushions to feel the excitement and realize that you're not alone—the flowers will support you.

## WEEK 6: Lavender

Get lavender. It doesn't matter if it's fresh or dried. The sweet scent of lavender is a symbol of the sweetness of life and a reminder of how important it is to appreciate our relationships with friends and family. You're allowed to celebrate and spend time with loved ones. Never forget that working hard to achieve our goals should never take the place of quality time with friends and family.

CHAPTER 3

# overcoming negativity

## CREMONS

The cremon flower has an unpretentious beauty that reminds us of the innocence we are all born with. When we're young, life is all about wonder—before the world steps in with its rules, control, and the endless *nos* that shape us and gradually strip away that innocence. But the cremon flower helps us reclaim those joyful memories. It's like the park swings you loved as a child, or laughter shared over a melting ice cream cone. Let these blooms remind you to rekindle friendships, eat s'mores with your kids, and smile more often, because life should still have moments of unfiltered joy, just like it did when you were young.

Magical Blooms is not your typical flower shop. Customers walk into a hip and eclectic studio-like shop, with flowers in unusual containers. I greet every customer with a warm smile and occasionally, because I am the demonstrative type, a warm embrace.

I am lucky to meet some amazing individuals while they're going through not-so-amazing times. It is through the medicine of flowers that I'm able to lift their spirits. When people are feeling down, that's when my work really starts. I can prescribe the specific flowers that will help them overcome darkness. You could be in the worst mood, but when you see uplifting flowers, such as sunflowers, gerbera daisies, or dahlias, they will make you smile.

## AMARANTHUS

The amaranthus flower is a symbol of turning intuition into action, a reminder that those random thoughts and sparks of inspiration are there for a reason—don't ignore them! We all have moments when an idea pops into our heads out of nowhere, nudging us toward something new and exciting. Whether it's planning the next big adventure, starting a business, or redecorating that room you've been thinking about, stop waiting and start doing. Get creative and clever with your life—grab an envelope and start saving for that dream trip to Italy, test drive the car you've always wanted, or go house hunting just for fun. I'm a big believer in vision boards because they help transform our ideas into reality. Amaranthus encourages you to keep your ideas in high vibration. Too often, we crush our passions with negativity or self-doubt—so instead, focus on thinking positively, trusting your intuition, and mastering the art of listening to your own dreams.

## Tulips: Healing from Addiction

There are so many varieties of tulips: parrot, French, feathered, and double-headed. They all have something in common: They are particular about their water intake. When you are dealing with a drug or alcohol problem, the tulip is a wonderful metaphor for your struggles. When you give a tulip too much water, it starts leaning over. It's quite interesting. Tulips also don't like to be bothered or touched. When you design with tulips, they like to be in an arrangement alone. When dealing with addiction, our friends tend to become isolated. Perhaps it's a toxic relationship you're addicted to? Perhaps it's a relationship that is not going anywhere, but for some reason you keep going back. Try relying on tulips. Their reaction to imbibing too much water can help you remember what happens to your body when it does the same with alcohol, drugs, or any other addiction. Tulips are also just a beautiful flower—the Dutch know what they're doing!

## COBRA LILY

Cobra lilies give off major *Little Shop of Horrors* vibes. Sadly, they're short-lived, drying up faster than you might like, but they're perfect for making a bold statement at any cool event. These flowers are stunning solo in a vase, with their merlot-colored veins weaving through white petals and hollow stems that almost look like they're from another world. Beyond their eye-catching beauty, cobra lilies are like negativity bouncers—they block out the bad vibes. Been around someone who's always whining, gossiping, or just plain negative? Maybe you're the one stuck in a grumpy mindset. Let cobra lilies absorb all that toxic energy and silence the negativity. They practically scream "Enough already!" It's time to cut the complaining and let these rare beauties bring in some fresh, positive air.

## Overcoming Social Media Overload

Overuse and dependence on social media can have a negative impact on your life. It's easy to compare yourself to others on Instagram or to covet an influencer's house, clothes, body, or marriage. This "compare and despair" can lead to a downward spiral of depression. The number one flower I prescribe to clients who are struggling with this feeling is the passion vine. As the owner of a business, I've gone through many highs and lows, and this flower has helped me a great deal. Since it's not available all year round, I recommend that clients display visuals of the passion vine around their home—on their bulletin board, taped to a mirror, as their screensaver, or on their smartphone's home screen. Having the visual on or near your electronic device can encourage you to become more mindful and remind you to stop comparing yourself to others and to stop thinking that you need more material things in your life to be happier. (If you cannot access passion vine, lavender holds parallel energy and can provide the same effect.)

## Overcoming Angst

Roses are associated with the heart chakra and have the highest vibration frequency for healing. Place red roses around your home to help. I love arranging them with chamomile, hydrangea, lavender (fresh or dried), rosemary, and mint. These wonderful combinations can combat anxiety when you're worrying about the future.

## Getting Over the Loss of a Romantic Relationship

If you or a friend is getting over the loss of a romantic relationship, it's best to have flowers next to your bedside. This will reassure and comfort you when you're alone at night. Yellows and whites are the best colors to put next to your bed when you're feeling down and depressed. They work to harmoniously uplift your energy, encourage you to fall in love with yourself, and give you the confidence that you're going to be okay.

## Self-Care

When you wake up in the morning, it's important to say "Good morning" to your soul. Place pink ranunculus on your bedside so you can see them as soon as you wake up. The medicine of the pink ranunculus reminds you to take care of your soul.

Self-care also means speaking to yourself in a positive way. If you see a photo of yourself or look in the mirror, be mindful of what you're saying to yourself. Having peach ranunculus around you will encourage you to speak kindly to yourself. You can be your own worst enemy, and these flowers will help clear the self-sabotage. Combine peach- and pink-toned ranunculus to create a feeling of joy in your home.

## Loneliness

The daffodil is comforting. It is the perfect medicine to help when you're feeling alone and needing someone to say "I'm here for you." When I first started Magical Booms, the daffodil was my logo. Its color and vibrancy are powerful. You want to buy daffodils extra tight; try not to buy them if they're already open, since they have a very short lifespan. Just like with daffodils, when you're feeling down and alone, you have to remember that feeling down doesn't last very long. All you have to do is pick up the phone and call a friend.

CHAPTER 4

# anxiety

Whether we like it or not, anxiety is a regular part of life. Regardless of what life stage you're in—you could be a student with final exams looming, a parent of a teenager who just started driving, or in a relationship with uncharted territory ahead—anxiousness can rear its head. Good news: Flowers can help! To help ease any form of anxiety, the number one flower I prescribe is chamomile—yes, the same chamomile we drink for tea.

You can find chamomile virtually anywhere all year round. Chamomile is powerful because its energies, fragrance, and message calm your nervous system. We drink chamomile tea to help soothe the stomach. In flower form, chamomile is a support system. The stem shoots up with multiple little flowers sprouting on it, like little fairy godmothers or angels. They're your cheerleaders, saying, "I'm here for you. I support you." If you have a deadline that you're trying to meet or if you're feeling anxious in a relationship and don't know where you stand—or if you're experiencing the extreme pressure of juggling too much—think of chamomile as your number one favorite friend. If you're looking for an alternative to chamomile, lavender can provide a quick pick-me-up for calming nerves (there's a reason why almost every spa you walk into is scented with lavender).

Chamomile is a member of the daisy family (it has daisy-like flowers budding on the stems). Daisies are synonymous with flower children—they are hippie-like and natural free spirits. Daisies never try too hard. They are the medicine that says, "You've got this." Chamomile comes in yellow button or white button, but daisy chamomile is ultimately the best flower for anxiety.

## How to Communicate with Chamomile

There is no wrong way to interact with chamomile. Just by placing chamomile all around your living space, you will feel better energetically, emotionally, and spiritually. Your anxiety will dissipate. When you're feeling super anxious, rub your fingers on it. You can smear it around your third eye or put your nose into the flower and take a deep breath. You can also keep the essence on your hand and take in the fragrance that way.

The core principles of chamomile are healing and soothing of the nervous system. Chamomile reminds you to breathe deeply and relaxes your mind. The cost of allowing anxiety to rule your life can be very high, and chamomile is an inexpensive flower to use to counteract that.

## Creating a Chamomile Arrangement

Clean the leaves off the chamomile stem and place it in water alone or pair it with lavender, rosemary, mint, roses, or spray roses, depending on the season. You can also use chamomile as a filler flower—like a baby's breath or a wax flower. Chamomile will help support other flowers. This is a somewhat full flower, so you need only a stem or two in any vessel to get the job done. Use a jar, a small bud vase, or your favorite container and let the medicines do their work.

## Where to Place Chamomile

Place chamomile in rooms and spaces in your house where stress and anxiety are most likely to surface. Many people experience anxiety when they're trying to sleep, when everything goes silent and your mind starts tripping out. When you wake up in a panic, chamomile is there to remind you that you're not alone. For this reason, the bedside is often the best place for chamomile. If you're working from home, place it on your desk or wherever you sit and do work. Chamomile has a similar property to mint; you will find that it destresses you and promotes a soothing feeling.

## Neighborhood Walk

I live in the most beautiful area of Palos Verdes, and walking my dog gives me great joy. One day, I was walking Valentine and turned the corner in one of my favorite areas, where there's an explosion of wildflowers, and came upon a teenager lying on the path, panicked and struggling to breathe. She was frantically waving at me. I asked her if she had any medical conditions, and when she said no, it occurred to me that she might be having a full-blown panic attack. She managed to tell me that she'd been so struck by this feeling on her run that she fell to the ground and legitimately thought she was dying. I pulled her into my arms and gave her a hug—as a mom myself, I know the power of a warm hug.

I gave her a flower that was nearby and told her to open her eyes to look at it and feel its textures, to try to bring her back to nature. I called her mom, and a couple of hours later, her mom texted me to say thank you. She told me that her daughter, who was only sixteen years old, had been stressed out studying for her AP exams. I told her to go to the store and immediately get some chamomile flowers to place around the house. I heard back from the mom a few days later, and she was happy to report her daughter was less stressed and seemed to be in a much better place.

## Social Anxiety

Social anxiety can affect us at any time—whether it's anticipating going to a party, a work function, or a family gathering. The feeling of fear that kicks in can be enough to make you want to crawl up in a ball and hide. The flowers you want to surround yourself with to help ease social anxiety are red roses, strawflower, paper daisies, and carnations. For example, consider combining red roses and strawflower; they are strong and powerful flowers that evoke a sense of belonging. Visualize a carnation at your third eye while walking into a crowd. It helps take the edge off. Strawflowers are very stable and ward off negativity. Remember that we don't need to be liked by everyone. The only person who really needs to like us is ourself.

Why is the combination of red roses and strawflowers so powerful for friendship and socializing? The red rose symbolizes love, strength, and unwavering commitment. When paired with strawflowers, known for their longevity, the message is one of lasting connection and loyalty. Together, they stand tall, making a bold statement—just like wearing red lipstick. Even if you're shy in social situations or you don't wear makeup, think about how striking and confident someone looks with red lips. It's bold, it's fearless, and it's captivating. Like the red rose and strawflower, this duo makes you feel powerful and magnetic. People are drawn to you—they want to work with you, refer you, and introduce you to their friends, and they're thrilled when you show up. Keep these flowers around as you get ready, and let them remind you of the energy they hold, because that boldness, beauty, and power? It's all you.

### VIBURNUM

Viburnum, sometimes called snowball, is a spring flower. It looks like a mini hydrangea on a wooden stem. It has a very short spring season. It is a great filler flower to use for a green tone in your designs and looks kind of droopy.

Viburnum supports you and helps you believe in yourself. Stop doubting. Wake up and put your thoughts into action! Write things down and get them out of your head. Circle what brings you the most joy and energy and tackle those ideas first. Nothing feels better than checking things off a list.

**ABOVE:** Lisianthus.

## Flowers for Teenage Angst

Being a teenager is a wild time in life. Hormones are raging, and there are so many ups and downs. Some moments you feel lonely and anxious, and other times you are filled with heartbreak and passion. I created a flower design that allows the hormones to do their thing and teens to soak up the love. Snapdragons offer support. Roses help the heart understand that you're just going through a phase. Gerbera daisies are for joy and to remind you to be happy and to not take everything so personally. Lisianthus allows you to accept that this time will pass, friends will change, and it's going to be okay. Mint is just to balance the design, but it also reminds us to breathe and helps us feel safe. A teen can keep these flowers next to their bedside or desk. The reading behind this arrangement is *Be your own best friend.*

## DIANTHUS: BE PRESENT

The flower industry brought out a new dianthus variety a few years ago with a stem that looks like a fresh stick of moss with no bloom, just green, called green trick. After seeing it on the farm a few times, I brought it into my flower shop and added it to designs. I was uncertain at first but eventually started to enjoy this flower because it tends to last the longest out of all the blooms in a mixed design. Dianthus's message is to let go of anxiety. When you are spending time with your kids, enjoy this time. If you have a friend visiting, take a pause from your other obligations. When you are cooking in the kitchen, enjoy the mess, smells, and flavors. Enjoy being around people and get off your phone, ignore email. It can all wait.

## Jenny's Strategy for Stage Fright

Not many people know this, but I get anxious before speaking in front of large groups of people. I give talks often now, but I still get butterflies in my stomach and experience slight panic attacks. Here's a little trick for you: If you are about to walk on stage to present or accept an award or to talk to a large audience, imagine that you are surrounded by sunflowers. The sunflower's sole purpose is to blast happiness and energy. Just imagine your head as a giant sunflower, and you will be smooth, calm, and in control on stage.

CHAPTER 5

# grief and loss

**ABOVE:** Lisianthus. • **OPPOSITE:** Clematis.

To live is to experience grief and loss. Maybe your friend suffered from a miscarriage, or their mom just passed away, or their husband has cancer. Or perhaps it was time to say goodbye to your dog after sixteen years of companionship. There are so many different reasons we grieve, and grief does not always mean death. Someone could be grieving the loss of their job, the loss of a best friend who moved out of the country, or even the loss of a time in their life they cherished. When there's a loss, you feel an emptiness in your heart. You can count on flowers to help fill you up and keep you going.

## Condolence Flowers Don't Have to Be Sad

It's common practice to send white orchids or lilies when there is a death, but I am not a fan of this custom. Orchids are somber and create even more sadness. Instead, I like to send a bloom that will lift some of the heaviness the mourner is feeling. Hot-pink roses are perfect for someone who needs a pick-me-up and an instant smile. Alstroemeria are known for having long-lasting blooms and are a good choice for someone who has suffered a loss—you don't want flowers that are going to die quickly.

In Mexico, for Day of the Dead, they give marigolds, which uplift the spirits and bring good vibrations. Scented geraniums are a wonderful mood booster for someone who doesn't want to get out of bed. Anything that could be freshly cut from a garden—such as mint, rosemary, hellebores, lavender, and ranunculus—are joyful flowers. If you're trying to create a tall design, mention to the florist that you'd like snapdragons, because they are playful flowers. Another great tall flower is larkspur, which sparkles with colors of purple, pink, and white. Eucalyptus is soothing to the soul and helps Zen out the body.

## MINI LILIES

Mini lilies are the perfect breakup and divorce flower—time to shake off the tears, dance, and reclaim your joy! Traditionally, lilies are seen as sympathy flowers, but these mini ones are here to wipe away the tears and remind you that sadness isn't forever. Place them in the corners of your home where sadness lingers, and let their beauty remind you to crank up the music, move your body, and embrace the celebration of life. Remember, this too shall pass, and you'll emerge stronger. They're a true "school of life" flower, reminding you that every moment—good or bad—teaches you something. Just keep in mind that when the lilies bloom, you will want to remove the pollen, because it can stain whatever it touches.

FLOWER℞

**Rad friend gift.** *Snapdragons, pincushion flowers, coxcomb, bunny tail, hanging amaranthus, kangaroo paws, trailing jasmine.*

## Flower Placement in the Home During Periods of Grief

If you're grieving, the best place to put flowers is on the kitchen counter, since this is the most active space in the house. Whenever you're feeling bummed and sad, look up, and the flowers will elevate your brain chemistry. Flowers help release serotonin and are natural antidepressants that help lift your mood when you're grieving. When you've just lost someone, it's okay to embrace your sadness and let the emotions flow—even if that means shedding tears. It can be hard to cry in front of others, but flowers are there to reassure and comfort you. When you're talking about the person who has passed, the presence of the flowers will help you release your emotions. Flowers are a visual representation of beauty, and beauty has an emotional effect on us.

If you are hosting a gathering for your friends and family, like a wake or a shiva, it's best to place the flowers in the center of the room.

## Grieving a Mother or a Father

For the death of a mother, I look for purples, whites, and yellows—colors that represent the softness of being a mother. For a father's passing, it would be wonderful to go with yellows, whites, or blues. My favorite blues are delphinium, hydrangeas, blue tweedia, muscari, and forget-me-nots. For purples, I favor sweet pea, lisianthus, and anemone.

FLOWERx

**Bedside cheer.** *Cremon mums, myrtle, mini calla lily, chrysanthemums.*

FLOWERx

**Positive mindset, clear head, seeing the positive in every outcome, good or bad.** *Sweet peas.*

## Add Fragrance

The sumptuous scent of fresh flowers works magic on our brain chemistry. The scent is refreshing, and fragrances can bring back joyful memories. When I smell jasmine, it reminds me of my grandma. I love to use white stock, lavender, or hellebores. When they're in season, sweet peas are wonderful to give to a friend who is grieving.

## SWEET PEAS

Sweet peas look like they are tears from heaven growing on thin stems. The fragrance they produce is sweet and delightful. Their colors are so pretty, too: lavender for healing, pink for gifting, white for bringing back your innocence, coral for playtime, and deep purple for condolences or health. Find a simple small vase and place sweet peas, mini calla lilies, cremons, or mums near your keyboard, in your bathroom, or on your kitchen sink. These flowers bring a sense of safety to your spiritual and physical space. They are a reminder that there is a higher power that will always make you feel protected.

## JENNY'S TIP

**For a child or teenager who is coping with loss, I like to give gerbera daisies (above) in any color, spray roses, or sunflowers, because they exude playfulness and can lighten the mood for a youngster in pain.**

OPPOSITE, CLOCKWISE FROM TOP LEFT: Lisianthus, trailing jasmine, hellebores, lisianthus.

FLOWERx

**Condolences.** *Gerbera daisies, marigolds, spray roses, chrysanthemums.*

## Condolence Flower Etiquette

I always recommend ordering a condolence arrangement in a container instead of wrapped. You don't know if the person is in distress or if they even have a vase that isn't already in use, and they won't want to deal with finding a vase for flowers in this state. It is better to send the flowers a day or two after the announcement of the death. Avoid sending them right away, because that's when people are hurting the most, and the flowers will likely go unnoticed. It's nicer to send flowers to the house as opposed to the place of worship or funeral home where the service is being held, so that the bereaved can enjoy them longer. It's always uncomfortable bringing flowers home after a service when you're emotionally drained and upset.

Many people don't know what to say on the card. Let the flowers speak for themselves and send the simplest card that lets them know you're thinking of them.

## Supporting a Grieving Coworker

One day when we were about to close, one of my coworkers, a young sweet woman named Lucy, received the call we all dread: Her brother had passed away. A bunch of us quickly created a beautiful, uplifting arrangement. We knew how alone and sad she must have been feeling, and the intention of the flowers was to give her a hug from our team.

## For the Death of a Pet

We love our pets fiercely. Unfortunately, there comes a time when our animals grow old and we have to say goodbye. If you find out your friend or neighbor is mourning their animal companion, one of the most thoughtful things you can do is to send flowers. A house can feel very empty after the death of a beloved pet. Don't go too big; it might upset them. A mixed seasonal bouquet is best in this instance. In spring, go with soft pastels; for fall, embrace warm, autumn tones; and in winter, choose a sweet and cozy pine mix. It's not about finding the perfect flowers–it's the thought and care behind acknowledging the loss of a beloved family member. Adding a heartfelt note about how much their pet will be missed is a simple but meaningful gesture.

## Magical Blooms Story

For many years, Tom, a retired and successful businessman, would come to the store three days before his anniversary to order red roses for his wife on their anniversary. Unfortunately, he passed away; in remembrance, their daughter, Caroline, uplifted her mom's sadness by continuing the tradition of sending roses with the kind message "You're adored," as though the spirit of her father was still giving her mother the flowers.

CHAPTER 6

# relationships

When I was a little girl, my grandpa would go to the grocery store every Friday to pick up flowers for my grandma. It was ceremonial and so special. I would come along with him, and he would always ask me which flowers looked good. He would almost always buy her red or white carnations—or, on occasion, red roses. We would put them in the cart, and as we checked out, I remember their fragrance. It was so romantic to watch my grandpa do this same routine every Friday over the many years they were married. Central to our health and happiness are the relationships in our lives. Flowers can help improve and sustain your relationships—and not just with romantic partners, either.

## The Power of Roses

It's hard not to talk about roses when thinking about romance and relationships. A lot of times, men come into the shop, and they just want to buy one single red rose. There's symbolism behind one red rose: It reminds us that it's not how big the bouquet is; it's the thought that counts. A single red rose is a simple and sweet way to say "I love you." Roses have the highest vibration of flower that exists on the planet, and they are embraced in ceremonies in different cultures around the world. This is because we are a vibration—just like water or music. If you're trying to work on the heart's desire or connecting to the heart, choose roses.

## Roses 101: A Complete Buyer's Guide

The rose represents the heart chakra and memories from the past.

**RED ROSES:** Red signifies a full commitment, one that communicates "I love you, and I am all in!" Red roses also help heal self-love. If you're going through a tough time in life and you can't control the external elements, buy red roses to help you fall back in love with yourself.

**YELLOW ROSES:** Yellow signifies friendship. It also represents freedom and abundance. Yellow will help lift someone up, so it is glorious for a get-well arrangement. Think of yellow as a blast of vitamin D to the heart.

**PINK ROSES:** Pink is an ideal shade to send to a friend. Pink roses bring excellence and magic to your life. Send pink roses to your friend if they just got engaged!

**PURPLE ROSES:** Purple is all about healing and calming yourself. If you suffer from migraines, purple roses will help. They also offer spiritual guidance: If you meditate, place purple roses around you, and they will help you listen to your own intuition.

**WHITE ROSES:** White evokes sophistication and classiness. They also help clear the mind—especially if you are worrying too much.

**ORANGE ROSES:** Orange has a caffeine-like vibe—it helps boost energy. It also helps clear misunderstandings with friends or business associates.

**PEACH ROSES:** Peach softens a room and creates a feeling of coziness.

**SPRAY ROSES:** This variety of rose offers support, especially when it has multiple flower heads, which feels like a group hug.

## Become a Rose-Buying Expert

When you call a florist or walk into a store, ask where their roses were grown. The best commercial roses are grown in Ecuador, due to the climate. Their rose heads are bigger, and their stems are stronger. California has beautiful David Austin roses, but they don't have as strong of a stem or as big of a head, and they have fewer petals. When you buy a rose, the head is not supposed to be super tight. You want the rose to be semi-open. If you buy them too tight, they may never open. On the other hand, you never want to buy a rose that's super open, because it won't last as long. Look at the stem; higher-quality roses have fewer thorns. If you see a few petals on the outside that look imperfect or are ripped, simply pull them off, and the rose will look brand new and unblemished. Depending on the rose, though, it can sometimes look more natural or organic to keep those imperfect petals.

## New Romantic Relationships: Pink or White Paper Daisies

When you receive pink or white paper daisies from the garden or from the farm, the petals are tight, similar to the shape of a Hershey's Kiss. At first, this bud looks a little disappointing—the edges are brown and lead up to a pink ball. Even the stems are not that pretty. But what's fascinating about paper daisies is that when they open, they remind us that little things can often be so sweet and magical. These flowers are perfect for when you first start dating and it's way too early in the relationship to give a red rose. Just like when a relationship blooms, the paper daisy opens up and becomes the most vibrant soul flower.

## GLADIOLUS

When buying gladiolus, go for stems with blooms that are still tight—it's exciting because you won't know their color until they open! If you buy them before they open, they can last a solid two to three weeks. Gladiolus look stunning solo in a tall vase. This is a classic, old-school flower that people either adore or dislike, but believe it or not, they're super romantic. When you're in love and committed, gladiolus make a perfect weekly addition to your space, serving as a visual reminder of the love in the air. And when your marriage feels stale or arguments flare up, take a deep breath, glance at the flowers, and remember why you fell in love in the first place.

## Spicing Things Up

Relationships can get stale. The question is, how do you spice things up when you feel like you're in a rut? When you see someone every day, it's easy to feel unappreciated or bored. You may even start picking fights.

Rice flowers tell you to knock it off! Return to the memory of when you first met that special someone and remember why you fell in love with them in the first place. The rice flower is great for relationship bonding and understanding how to refresh and add some zest when things feel stale. If you put rice flowers around, it will encourage you to be creative and come up with new ways to reinvent yourself. It reminds you that it's not up to the other person to revive a relationship—it's up to both of you!

## Friendship Flowers

### DAHLIAS

Dahlias are the best to give to someone you love. They are the friendship flower. Whether you've just met someone you feel a connection to or you have a friend you've known for forty years, give them dahlias to convey a floral hug, affection, and smile. The mouthwatering colors stimulate your emotions. There are multiple dimensions to this flower—layers of joy, textures of stories, and a freedom that comes from each color allowing itself to stand out. This is also what friendship is all about. Some dahlias last a long time, and others fizzle out quickly. Some are louder, and others are quieter. Dahlias are a reminder to cherish your friendships.

Certain friends remain in your life for the long haul. These are the ones you instantly click with and right away feel like you've known them forever (maybe they were in your past life). My favorite flowers to prescribe for your ride-or-die are dahlias and sweet peas combined in a ceramic vase. Dahlias and sweet peas send a message that says "I'm so excited to be your friend and I enjoy your company. I will always support you." Maybe you don't talk to this friend every day—in fact, maybe it's a friend you speak to only a couple times a year, but you know that this person has your back, and you have theirs. When you get older and move or get married and have kids, friendships can fade away, but flowers can be the glue that holds your friendship together. When was the last time you randomly reached out to a friend and sent them flowers? There is no better time to start.

## Group Hug!

Here's a super feminine and girly design that acts as a support system, just like your group of friends. It's the flower equivalent of a group hug. There are multiple color roses that represent the heart chakra and symbolize talking softly and kindly through the heart. Lavender is for healing. Veronicas are for flirting (it can be fun to flirt with your friends!). Trailing jasmine is for romance. Rosemary is for savoring the occasions and to brush off drama. Keep the bouquet low profile, a height you can have conversations over, even if you're only able to converse over the phone. This is to help you feel the energy of your girlfriends in the room, even if they're not with you. Even if you're all busy in life, it feels like you are all hanging out together.

## My Favorite Friendship Flowers

The best flower colors to give to our friends are yellow, white, and pinks—either bright pinks or soft pinks, depending on the emotion. Most of the customers who come into the flower shop love peonies. In addition to dahlias, I also like to prescribe Stargazer lilies, spray roses, hydrangeas, or an orchid. A mixture of white tweedia, baby's breath, hellebores, and roses is always nice on an outdoor table where friends gather.

**SPRAY CARNATIONS** are timeless, yet they are always reinventing themselves with vibrant, modern colors. Just like friendships, they are long-lasting. They're the perfect flower for celebrating both the highs and the lows with those closest to you, always standing by your side. With real friends, you can be your authentic self, have honest conversations, and share every victory and defeat with the same sense of trust and joy that these carnations symbolize.

**GERBERA DAISIES** will make your friend feel happy inside—they are the flower equivalent to a big smile!

**ANEMONES** are everyone's best friend. I call them the BFF flower. Everyone loves them! They're white with black centers, a reminder of something fresh, hip, and delightful. Buy them at harvest time and check that the blossom is tight so they will last longer.

**PAPER DAISIES** are super fun and very playful. They're the type of flowers that say, "Do you want to hang out and get a mani/pedi or lunch?" They have an interesting shape to them—large heads shoot all the way up to a small head.

**LISIANTHUS** are durable flowers, kind of like a friendship. This why I relate them to long-lasting friendships.

**YELLOW OR PINK ROSES** represent a divine feminine energy. They put your friend on a pedestal and communicate that you adore and respect them. Roses are like soft-spoken words. Just make sure to purchase them when they're tight, so they last longer.

**PROTEAS** are powerful, long-lasting flowers that remind your friend that you have not forgotten about them. When I use them in arrangements, it's meant to evoke this.

FLOWER$_x$

**Happiness and comfort.** *Gerbera daisies, mini carnations, mint, hypericum (aka coffee beans).*

**ABOVE, CLOCKWISE FROM TOP LEFT:** Lisianthus, protea, veronica, paper daisy. • **OPPOSITE:** Anemone.

FLOWER℞

**A casual thank-you to the host of a gathering.**
*Dahlias, paper daisies, orlaya, roses, baby's breath, dusty miller, tweedia, hellebores.*

## Snapdragons: The Ultimate Symbol of Friendship

When snapdragons are in a field, they stand up for one another. Regardless of their color, they are all the same height, and they grow close and support one another like soldiers. Snapdragons remind us to surround ourselves with people who have the same values and let go of the ones who are no longer serving us. If a snapdragon is in a field by itself, it would snap in half because of the wind, but when a row of snapdragons prop each other up, they may sway slightly to one side, but they are there for each other.

## When It's Your Turn to Say "I'm Sorry"

It's not fun to admit when you've upset someone, especially someone you've been friends with for many years. One of the nicest things you can do when you've upset a friend is to send flowers. I love alstroemerias, which are friendly and playful. I often add some softness to the arrangement with white tweedia and garden roses in jewel tones in a fun container. The arrangement should be playful, just like your relationship. We all make mistakes or say the wrong words sometimes, so just say you're sorry and send flowers.

## You: Bring Back the Magic

For years, I stayed away from buying tweedia because it doesn't last for more than a day. It also has a milky stem, which can make the water look very murky. It was a hard no for years until I saw this magical, fairylike flower at its peak. It transported me back to a time of innocence in my life—before anyone yelled or got angry with me. When I was a kid, our entire family would go to Disneyland once a year. We would arrive right when the gates opened and stay until the park closed. It was a place to escape from reality, use your imagination, and spend the day, no matter what your age.

Tweedia helps me remember how important it is to protect my son's innocence and how important it is to infuse magic into our children's lives. I was enamored of the movie *Alice in Wonderland* and especially loved the part when Alice shrinks. She becomes the same size as the flowers, and they start talking to her, each one with a distinct personality. I would rewind that part over and over again.

When I became a mom, I made a choice to change the pattern of yelling that reaches back generations in my family. Jack has never had a time out, and I would never consider hitting him or hurting him emotionally. Tweedia wants you to take a hard look and decide which patterns we want to carry on and which we want to stop for the health of our own family.

FLOWER$_x$

**For someone celebrating new beginnings or getting over the hump.** *Garden roses, sage, hellebores, alstroemeria, tweedia.*

## JENNY'S TIP

I am often asked if there are flowers that evoke romance besides roses. The answer is *absolutely!* Lilacs are one of my favorite romantic flowers, along with dianthus, kiwi vines, rosemary, kangaroo paws, hellebores, trailing jasmine, hanging amaranthus in red (above right), strawflowers, bunny tail, and proteas (above left). Sometimes people relate romance to their loved one's favorite flower. My advice is to find out your sweetheart's favorite flower and pair it with roses to make it truly romantic. I think flowers with an alluring fragrance, like hyacinth, are also very romantic.

FLOWERx

**A pulse of energy and confidence.** *Dahlias, proteas, dianthus green trick, bunny tail, hellebores, fire coxcomb, yarrow, billy balls, rosemary, trailing jasmine, kangaroo paws.*

CHAPTER 7

# wellness

## Passiflora Passion Vine

I was horseback riding in Palos Verdes when I first laid eyes on the passiflora passion vine. I describe it as an outer galactic, cosmo planet flower. There are a few varieties. People ask me, "What is your favorite flower?" This is the one! It is an antidepressant flower. It helps you stay positive and opens your mind and soul to remind you to always look for the blessing in any circumstance. When something happens that throws you off, the passiflora passion vine encourages you to look at the situation in a different way. How can I learn and grow from this? How can I also avoid making this same error or experiencing this same feeling again?

I recently had pneumonia for the first time in my life. My doctor said I needed to rest and slow down. When you get sick, excitement and energy are stolen from your body. A layer of depression comes on when you're not feeling well. You must put your life on hold. Flowers are nature's antidepressant, and they are essential to your well-being. This is why it's so important to have nature around you when you're dealing with an illness—and even when you're not sick. If you continually nurture yourself with flowers, you are creating a lifestyle of wellness. If you are heartbroken, are experiencing menopause, or need to get through a series of medical treatments, you will want a steady stream of flowers to nourish you. Place them in every room, even the bathroom. You always need flowers around you to help support your wellness.

## BILLY BALLS: HAVE FUN

When we become adults and are married with kids and careers, sometimes we forget to have fun. Maybe we laughed on our first few dates with our lovers and enjoyed our kids, but then life became so darn stressful. Having to clean up, pay bills, organize—there's a heaviness to it all. Billy balls are all about tuning in to your kid-like energy. They are fun, zany-looking flowers. They will inspire you to take bike rides, swing on a swing, and if you're near the pool, instead of sitting next to it, swim in it and get your hair wet. Hear a song you like? Get up and dance. Here is my suggestion: Toss a colorfully wild pillow on the couch and place billy balls around the house to remind you to incorporate fun into your life.

FLOWER[x]

**To show a unique, rare, funky person that you see them.** *Spider mums, pincushion flowers, Mokara orchids, succulents, scabiosa pods, lily grass, billy balls, dogwood, Agonis.*

## Rat's Tail: Embrace the Weird

I add rat's tail as an extra to my design, an aftermath of play. Just when I think the design is complete, I add it at the last minute for a little bit of weirdness to make the design look different. Rat's tails are conversation starters because most people don't even know what they are looking at.

Rat's tails stand tall and have an odd texture. They are almost like a mixture of an amaranthus and an astilbe. These are seasonal spring or early-summer flowers. They come in mainly pinks and sometimes white. This flower tells us that it's okay to be a little off and embrace the weird.

## KALE: OVERCOMING NEGATIVE THINKING

Kale is one of my favorite plants to include in my designs. Ornamental kale, also known as flowering kale, is not the same type of kale you find in the grocery store. Its ruffled leaves come in beautiful shades of purple, pink, white, and green. Kale is hardy and resilient—it can withstand and even thrive in chilly fall and winter temperatures, sometimes becoming more vibrant as the weather becomes colder.

### Kale

Kale is one of the toughest plants, so it's great to have around if you are striving to be healthier. I used to be intimidated at the gym, with all these super-fit people around me working out. To relieve this negative thinking, I planted kale by the front entrance of my home, and every time I see it, I become my own coach, saying, "I get to work out." Now I use this "I get to…" phrasing in every area of my life and everything I do. Our body is our engine—what we think, eat, and surround ourselves with impacts our future. Kale is a team player, and it helps encourage us to keep going, thanks to its hardiness.

## Magical Blooms Story

A professional-looking man in his mid-thirties walked into the shop. I greeted him with a warm welcome, just as I do with everyone who enters. He asked me if we had any premade flower arrangements. I explained to him that we don't, but we make beautiful farm-fresh designs, and it takes me just a few minutes to create them. I said, "Let me know who the arrangement is for, and I'll make you something gorgeous." He looked around and paused. I reassured him and told him not to worry. "You came to the right shop. I'm the Flower Doctor, and I can help you." He looked me in the eyes and said, "Well, my mom just found out she has cancer and has less than a month to live. These are my farewell flowers to her."

My heart sank. But this is also when my abilities as the Flower Doctor really come into play. I told him not to worry and dashed to my cooler. I knew only the best flowers would do for this young man, who was clearly in a state of emotional shock and distress. I chose lisianthus in as many soothing and tranquil tones as possible and purple alyssum, along with purple kale, trailing jasmine that smelled like perfume, umbrella fern, white hydrangea, quicksand roses, mint, scabiosa, cedar, and dusty millers, and I arranged them in a small vase with fern textures for his mother's bedside—warm, silent love.

As I was creating this arrangement, I started talking to him because I could see that he was choked up. He could have gone anywhere, but he came to me. I was channeling energy, and I told him I could feel that his mom is very proud of him. As I gave him the arrangement, I had a message for him. I said that it doesn't feel like he had the best relationship with his mom, but it can be healed with the help of these flowers. I told him to place the flowers at her bedside, smile at her, look her in her eyes, and tell her, "I love you, Mom." I told him to let her feel that energy, and that every time she looks at the flowers, she'll feel his energy. Tears streamed down his face, but I could tell that this prescription was going to help heal their relationship.

## Why Sending Flowers Is the Best Medicine Around

It was 9:30 p.m. on shabbat, and I picked up the phone at my shop. On the other end was Mr. Matthews, one of my first clients. I hadn't heard from him in years. He was calling to tell me that his daughter had just been diagnosed with aggressive ovarian cancer. He asked if I could go visit her in the hospital. Of course, I said yes. Even though it had been almost a decade since I had seen her, I knew how meaningful it would be.

When you find out someone you care about is ill, it doesn't matter how long it has been since you've seen them or the status of your relationship. When you get that news, you must communicate to that person how much you care. The number one thing you can do is give someone your time by visiting them. It doesn't matter how big the bouquet is, but don't walk in the door empty-handed. If this person lives far away from you, sending flowers is essential. It can be a simple bud vase as an expression of love and appreciation.

## Flowers for Illness

When sending flowers to someone who is ill, keep it simple—nothing with too much fragrance. Soft-toned roses carry two vibrations of color to help boost the immune system—I love pinks and purples. Yellow roses are known for friendship and abundance and are a blast of vitamin D to the heart. For flowers that help any illness, I love the comfort of eucalyptus, lavender, roses, yarrow, amaranthus, strawflower, tansy, cotton yarrow, mints, and rosemary.

FLOWERx

**Nurturing, healing, and calm.**
*Misty blue, stock, dried lavender, mint, gunni, roses.*

FLOWER℞

**For a spiritual warrior to remove negativity.** *Chinese lanterns, sedum, hydrangeas, sage, marigolds, feather eucalyptus.*

## Best Blooms for Your Own Wellness

Lean more toward yellow, whites, and greens when selecting flowers for your own well-being. Much of the time I add orange or purple to the arrangement for support. The orange and purple flowers might feel a bit cartoonish at first glance, but they hold a deeper meaning—they represent royalty and remind us to level up and be bold. Think marigolds, roses, ranunculus, alstroemeria, sweet peas, lisianthus, anemones, hydrangeas, and orchids. These blooms remind us that life doesn't always go as planned. You push forward, but setbacks happen. Perhaps you thought you'd be more successful by now—married by twenty-nine, own a house by thirty, have a baby by thirty-five. But life has its own timing, and sometimes you just have to laugh at the unexpected. What if, instead of stressing, you allowed yourself to be happy and content where you are *right now*? Divorces happen. People get sick. Dream jobs sometimes require you to uproot. Constantly being hard on yourself or comparing your life to others will only drag you down. This combination of orange and purple is a testament to life's unpredictability and resilience—it's a reminder to embrace the journey, not just the destination.

**ABOVE, CLOCKWISE FROM TOP LEFT:** Cognac dahlia, blush dahlia, garden rose, sweet pea, misty blue, bicolor dahlia, baby blue eucalyptus (spiral eucalyptus).

CHAPTER 8

# designing with flowers

flowers have the power to alter our moods and brighten our days. They flood you with positivity and make you feel better emotionally, spiritually, energetically, and aesthetically. When you walk into your house, there should always be fresh flowers. Flowers are often considered a luxury, but in many ways, you can't afford *not* to have them when you realize how much they can help with your emotional state. When you have all this beauty around you—whether you're walking your dog and looking at people's gardens or checking out the flowers at the farmers market—it's easier to fight depression and anxiety.

Start thinking about buying flowers in the same way you purchase your produce, by focusing on what's in season: peonies in the spring; sunflowers and dahlias in the summer; and marigolds, liquid maple leaves, rose hips, and mums in the fall. Winter brings delicious pinecones, evergreens, white roses, and ilex berry. Flowers can last anywhere from two days to two weeks, depending on the type of flower, how fresh they are, and their care and environment. Once you read my tips (page 142), you will have a deeper understanding of how to get the most out of the flowers you purchase.

FLOWERx

**Congratulations!**
*Garden roses, dusty miller, spray roses, hellebores, paperwhite narcissus.*

## Peonies

Throughout the year, I get tons of calls from men asking, "Do you have peonies? It's her favorite flower." Peonies are gorgeous, timeless, and just a bit rare—they add a touch of luxury to everyday life. Their fragrance is another draw—peonies emit a sweet, fresh scent that's hard to resist. Their relatively short blooming season adds to their exclusivity; they're not available year-round, so when they do appear, it feels special. Peonies come in hues of pinks, white, yellow, coral, peach, and red/merlot tones. This flower helps to ease anger—when you look at peonies and see how beautiful they are, it softens the feeling of being upset. When they open, they mesmerize your eyes and open your heart.

I'm always bringing flowers to people. Unlike bringing a bottle of wine that will be finished by the time the party's over, when you bring someone flowers, you are leaving your spirit in the room.

### JENNY'S TIP

**If you've never been to someone's home, stick to neutral colors for flowers. Also, when bringing flowers to a party, never give a bouquet that's wrapped; always bring it in a vase. The hosts are probably busy welcoming guests and most likely won't have time to make a mess in the kitchen putting it in a vase themselves.**

## Grasses and Textures

It's super fun to add grasses to your designs for texture—think of it like cooking in the kitchen and adding a spice at the last minute. There are so many types of grasses: zebra, lily, bear, fountain, and more. For interesting textured stems, look for bunny tail and rattlesnake grass. Grasses look good even solo in a vase. As long as you have water in the vase, grass will last a long time.

Grasses remind us that not everything is as it appears. They are beautiful but often sharp, and if you touch them, they can cut. Sometimes when you look at a photo on social media, you might start assuming and comparing and feeling like your life sucks. The fantasy is that someone else's life is better than yours. The truth is, though, that the grass is *not* greener on the other side. Focus on watering your own grass.

## The 10 Rules of Design

I believe everyone is born a designer. All you need are the right skill sets and tools. Designing flowers is a form of therapy and a magical way to evoke creativity. Floral arrangement gives you an opportunity to feel like a kid again. You can tap in to the energy of being creative. As adults, we're often stuck at our desks, or we're expected to be so serious all the time. Playing with flowers is like playing in the sand at the beach. You're encouraged to get your hands dirty, and it's good for the soul. The colors, textures, and fragrances engage all of your senses. Flower arrangements should not be perfect. Don't be afraid to add flowers without thinking. The following are my cardinal rules of floral design that I teach at Magical Blooms—they're easy to follow and promise to bring out the budding designer inside you. Organize your flowers, put on inspiring music, and get in a good mood. I guarantee you will have the most beautiful showstopper of an arrangement!

**Rule 1:** Make sure you're present before you start designing. The goal is to have fun. All day long, we're hard on ourselves, but this is the time let go and enjoy some flower therapy. Channel the energy of why you're arranging the flowers. Is it for a friend? A birthday? For yourself? Visualize where the flowers are going. When you design, make sure you're standing, not sitting. This way, when you're playing with the flowers and you're rotating them, you will have complete control of your design. You don't want to be in a rush. Carve out about an hour—which is the same amount of time as a typical therapy session. Give yourself enough time to play and enjoy and allow the flowers to uplift you and increase your energy.

**Rule 2:** Put on your favorite mood-lifting music and comfortable shoes to keep you stable. Music is essential while designing. When I traveled to Holland with my son, we walked into a greenhouse filled with huge hydrangeas and orchids. The Dutch growers told me they would play classical music to their flowers to help them grow; I think that is genius. More people need to understand the connection between music and flowers. Flowers can feel the vibrations of the music, just like they can sense wind or rain. Playing music while you design allows you to feel the connection to the vibrations of the music and the flowers.

**Rule 3:** Consider where these flowers are going in your home, which will help you imagine the energy you want them to give off. For example, do you want the flowers in the kitchen? On the dining room table? Perhaps in your entryway or maybe at your bedside? Visualize the flowers in the vessel. Do you know where these flowers are going to be placed? Against a wall or on a table? If they will be placed against a wall, it's best to design the flowers from the front. For a table, where you see all sides of the vase, design from every angle. Don't go crazy when buying a container—the fancier the container, the more it will compete with the flowers. I like to keep it simple when choosing the vase. Consider whether to use a clear vase or an opaque container. When you're just getting the hang of flower designing, I recommend going with an opaque white container so that no one will be able to see the bottoms of the stems. An opaque container also will conceal any potentially murky water. To determine the size of your container, think about where the flowers are going to sit. If they will be placed on the kitchen counter, the container should be on the larger side. If it's for your bedside table or your desk, go with a smaller vessel.

**Rule 4:** Lay out all your tools. Just like chefs have their mise en place, floral designers need to have their tools in front of them. You will need a vase full of water, binding wire, a sturdy pair of choppers or cutters, a brick of floral foam, and tape or chicken wire. Consult online sources and websites to buy the most efficient tools (I suggest that you read the reviews, which are more helpful than the company's description).

**Rule 5:** Inspect the stems and remove any dead leaves or dead petals. Organize by piling the same type of flowers together, such as roses, gerbera daisies, and mums. Do the same with greens, like eucalyptus. Your flower design feels more organized and focused if you concentrate on one type of flower category at a time.

**Rule 6:** Less is more when trimming stems. Start conservatively—you can always cut off more of the stem, but if you cut too much, it won't grow back. When you cut the flower, you must make sure the stem is long enough to hit the bottom of the vase. If it doesn't hit the bottom of the vase, that flower will die sooner than the others. Try to have the flowers next to the vase so you can measure as you cut. If the flower stems don't reach the bottom of the vase, you can place a balled-up plastic grocery bag or plastic wrap on the bottom.

**Rule 7:** Make sure the vase is filled 75 percent with water. The flowers are their thirstiest during the first twenty-four hours. When you refill the vase, you won't need as much water.

**Rule 8:** Line up the flowers in your workspace, including the greenery and filler. Always start by adding one type of greenery at a time to the vase, and then move on to the next type of greenery. If you have extras, put them aside. Once you have the foundation of greenery in place, move on to the flowers. Start with the biggest flower first, then move on to the second biggest, and so on. The filler flower should be last.

**Rule 9:** I always design my arrangements using a lazy Susan. I put the vase right in the center and turn it as I work; this helps me see the arrangement from all angles and fill any empty spots with holes as I go. Working this way gives me complete control of the design.

**Rule 10:** After you place the arrangement in its designated spot, don't forget to rotate it regularly. You don't want the flowers to remain in one position. Play with the design and twist it around throughout the day or every other day. This will show off all the beautiful flowers!

## FILLER FLOWERS

### *Baby's Breath*

Baby's breath now comes in fun colors—hot pink, turquoise blue, lemon yellow—dyed to match your mood or a special occasion. During the holidays you can add some to your Christmas tree or use them on your mantel with twinkle lights—it looks so pretty!

### *Queen Anne's Lace*

A delicate wildflower often dismissed as a roadside weed, Queen Anne's lace exudes a quiet grace that brings an organic, Victorian elegance to floral arrangements. Drought-resistant and always in season, it's the perfect filler for creating a soft, natural style. Its angelic, airy presence invokes a sense of peace and protection, like being cradled by unseen hands. It may leave a trail of tiny petals, a gentle reminder to let go of control, relax, and embrace life's fleeting moments.

### *Chocolate Lace*

With its merlot, mauve, and white tones, chocolate lace brings warmth and comfort to designs. It reminds us that even in tough times, everything will be okay.

## Cheat Sheet: Tape Grids and Floral Oasis

Tape grids offer a way to give you control of your flowers so they don't fall over in the arrangement. A grid will not work well if you're using a round or an irregularly shaped container, so use a 5- or 6-inch-wide square or rectangular container. Use floral tape to create a tic-tac-toe-like grid with equal-sized boxes on the top surface of the vase. Don't worry—the flowers will cover up the tape. Add water *after* you create the grid; if you fill the vase with water beforehand, the tape may not stick well and you'll get frustrated. Place flowers into each box in the grid; this will separate them and prop them up.

You can also use a brick of floral foam, which helps stabilize flowers and keeps them in place. Don't completely fill the container with foam—leave extra room so that you can fit big, chunky stems like sunflowers into the open spots.

## Best Flower Cutters/ Choppers

I remember buying my first Japanese choppers on Abbot Kinney Boulevard, a hipster street in Venice Beach, California. I thought I was so cool. I was convinced that an expensive pair of cutters would make me a better designer. That was a silly thought. In fact, those choppers landed me in the hospital when I was showing off in my store. After creating thousands of designs, I work at an unusually fast pace—I can typically make an arrangement in less than two minutes. As you can imagine, on that occasion, a good tune was playing and I was dancing, and the next thing I saw was blood—my left thumb was cut pretty deep. My friend Zosia, who worked with me for twelve years, called 911.

The tool you use is *not* about the price—it's about how comfortably it fits in your hand and the requirements of the flower you are cutting. Some cutters are stiff and some are springy, so you'll have to decide what feels best to you and works well for what you're cutting. I know many people who buy tools based on the brand alone, while others buy tools because they're on sale or they like the color. My advice is to look for something at a mid-range price: very cheap tools will be crappier, but very expensive tools won't necessarily perform better.

## JENNY'S TOP TIPS FOR BUYING CUT FLOWERS

When you buy flowers from a florist shop or grocery store, as opposed to buying from a farmers market, they have probably been sitting for a while. Take your time and inspect them to make sure their stems are strong and the flower itself isn't wilting. Be choosy.

- Whenever possible, buy directly from a flower farm or a quality source that buys directly from flower farms. This means purchasing flowers from a farmers market or from a shop or website, like Magical Blooms, that clearly states that their flowers come directly from a farm.
- While buying flowers directly from a farm is the best way to ensure that your flowers are fresh and will last longer, there is no shame in buying them from the grocery store on occasion, especially for a quick fix.
- Always inspect the flower for brown marks and make sure the head is not sad or droopy. Check to see if the stem feels squishy or strong.
- The powdered flower food that comes with store-bought flowers tends to get gunky and sit on the bottom of the vase, and it can turn the water murky. I prefer using clear liquid flower food or simply changing the water daily.
- If you are buying flowers in the grocery store, you can never go wrong with chrysanthemums. I would avoid hydrangeas, as they will likely die quickly.
- All roses must be stored in a cooler. If you see roses sitting out, not in a cooler, do not buy them! Look closely at the head of the rose and make sure it's not squishy and doesn't feel like it's going to snap off.
- Avoid the flowers sitting by the door at the grocery store when it's warm outside. You're better off buying flowers located in the floral department of a larger grocery store.
- Always ask your florist to make you a fresh arrangement. Buying a premade arrangement is similar to going to the grocery store and buying a premade sandwich that has been sitting around for hours—or days. The bread is soggy, and the lettuce is wilted. When you walk into a flower shop, ask for a fresh design. Don't go over to the cooler and buy one that's already made.

# ACKNOWLEDGMENTS

Jack Golden Barker, my son. If I were to have ordered you from the universe, you would be exactly what I dreamed of. You were raised in a flower shop. You have seen me handle all sorts of business transactions. You are my true flower. Thank you for allowing me to work lots of hours. You're positive and helpful! It's an honor to be your mother and watch you grow. The best decision I ever made was being a single mother to you.

My investors Rajesh Duggal, Joe Rust, and Mitch Grossman. I wouldn't have been able to make business moves without you!

My mom, Janet Barker. Thank you for allowing me to be an independent woman at such a young age. You taught me how to pretend and to enjoy being resourceful when I was little.

I would have never written this book if it weren't for my dad, James Carson. Before he passed away, he told me that I was going to write a book. I looked at him and replied, "I don't write." It was the consistency of his encouragement that inspired me to start writing.

Special thanks to my writing partner, Melissa Schweiger.

Kirsten and Jim Buch, for being dear friends who helped me grow the business and invited me to meet other business opportunities and expand my visions.

Dr. John Putman and Glen Rogers, my dear landlords. They believed in me when I was twenty-three years old and have never left my side!

My sweet grandfather Jack Barker, for being glued to my side and raising me—always making sure that I was happy and smiling and being my best friend.

I'm so grateful for my branding agent Dan Levin from Prominent Brand+Talent. I remember the first day we met—I was so nervous. By the second day, he already had a contract ready for me. At first, I didn't understand why he even wanted to work with me, but his belief in me has helped me grow and expand the business. Dan never left my side through highs and lows. He is an amazing cheerleader for me. I'm so grateful to have him in my life as a friend, along with his wife, Lisa. I love them both to pieces and am so grateful.

Special thanks to my book agent Eileen Cope at the Cope Media Group. I remember when Dan and I were sending off emails to agents, trying to figure out how to pitch our book, and Eileen was the first person to respond in less than twenty minutes. She wrote back in all caps "I LOVE JENNY BARKER!!!" It's such an honor to have one of the best New York book agents helping me create this book. Eileen has been such a pleasure and a dream to work with. I'm so grateful to have her as my book agent and consider her a great friend now. I'm looking forward to many more books!

I would love to thank Shannon Kelly and Sara Bader, my editors, for being so delightful. I'm so appreciative—they've been dream editors to work with. They've made this a better book. I'd also like to thank Melanie Gold, Susan Van Horn, Seta Zink, Amy Cianfrone, and the whole Running Press team.

# THE APOTHECARY

For your reference, here is a list of many of the plants and flowers I draw on and their uses.

Acacia—removal of narcissism

Acacia, finger—immunity

Acacia, flowering—disengaging from passive-aggressive behavior

Acacia, green feather—clearing negative attitudes

Acacia, purple feather—establishing boundaries

Agonis foliage—fierce determination

Agrostemma—angelic spirit

Allium—protection from others

Alstroemeria—support

Amaranthus—embracing the unknown

Amaryllis—uplifting spirits

Ammi majus (false Queen Anne's lace)—self-confidence

Ammi majus, chocolate—love

Anemone—protection, friendship

Berzelia—strength in challenging circumstances

Bird of paradise—power in business

Bougainvillea—vibrancy

Boxwood, royal—trust

Bupleurum—cherishing a moment

Calendula—cheering on others

Calla, mini (stems)—serious focus

Campanula, medium—spiritual energy

Carnation—consistency and stability

Cedar incense—speaking more kindly

Celosia wheat—clearing narcissism

Chamomile—healing and self-care

Cherry blossom—prosperity

Chrysanthemum—support

Chrysanthemum, China—removing social anxiety

Cornflower—laughter

Cosmos, chocolate—meditation

Coxcomb—clearing narcissistic energy

Craspedia (billy balls)—discipline

Crocosmia—fiery energy

Daffodils—clearing loneliness

Dahlia—ultimate friendship

Daisy, killian and shasta—free spirits

Deflexus—angelic fairy energy

Delphinium, belladonna—boosting memory

Dianthus, gypsy—consistency

Dogwood, flowering—dreaming

Dusty miller—forgiveness

Echinacea—wellness

Echinops (thistle)—spiritual protection

Eriostemon, budded—chakra alignment

Eucalyptus—resting and healing

Fern—psychic protection

Feverfew (chamomile)—sleep

Foxglove digitalis—dedication

Freesia—protection from bullies

Gardenia—reflection

Geranium—meditation

Gerbera daisy—bringing more joy

Geum, mango and red—learning new skills

Gomphrena—socializing

Grass—changing up routines

Grevillea—removing bully energy

Heather—new beginnings

Hellebore—healing heartbreak

Honey bracelet—self-kindness

Hydrangea—communication

Hypericum (coffee bean)—honesty

Iris—evoking memories

Ivy bush—fond memories

Jasmine, trailing—relieving panic attacks

Kale, flowering—healthier choices

Kangaroo paws—manifesting

Kiwi vine—creative energy

Lamb's ear—calmness

Larkspur—intuition

Lavender—balance

Leatherleaf—positivity

Leucadendron, Rising Sun—power

Leucadendron, Safari Sunset—confidence

Leucadendron, Winter Sunshine—growth

Leucospermum pincushion—supporting the immune system

Lily, Casa Blanca—trust

Lisianthus—grace

Luma—humility

Magnolia—sophistication

Marigold—reducing stress

Millet—motivation

Mint—calm

Misty blue—lifting frequencies

Monterey cypress—energy boosts

Myrtle—taking the higher ground

Myrtle, mini—solving problems

Narcissus—enjoying fond memories

Nigella—quieting your mind

Okra pods—nutrition

Olive branches—old soul energy

Olive branches, fruited—holiness

Orchid, cymbidium—stability

Orchid, phalaenopsis—clearing clutter

Orchid, white—lifting emotions

Oregano—engagement

Orlaya—relieving social anxiety

Ornithogalum (star of Bethlehem)—connecting to soul

Paper daisy—embracing innocence

Paperwhites—evoke memories from past

Passion vine—healing depression

Peony—clearing anger

Pine, juniper—feeling more settled

Pine, ponderosa—creating traditions

Pini aussi—embracing new horizons

Pitt—joyful music

Poppy, hybrid—hidden secrets

Protea, Pink Ice—confidence

Pumpkin tree—enjoying holidays with fun

Quince, flowering—beauty

Ranunculus—joy

Redwood—happiness and devotion

Rice flower—devotion

Rose, garden—slowing down

Rose, orange—boosting energy

Rose, peach—creating warmth

Rose, pink—evoking femininity

Rose, purple—intuitive spiritual guidance

Rose, red—healing the heart

Rose, spray—support

Rose, white—reducing anxiety

Rose, yellow—getting well

Rose hip—setting boundaries

Rosemary—joy

Ruscus Israel—stability

Safflower—spiritual healing

Salal—happiness

Scabiosa scoop—joy

Sedum—soul

Smilax—religion

Snapdragon—playfulness

Solidaster—focus

Statice—celebrating old friendships and your uniqueness

Stephanotis—relaxing

Stock—releasing grieving

Stock, purple—healing

Strawflower—relieving social anxiety

Sumac—clearing abuse

Sunflower—getting well

Sweet pea—self-kindness

Tulip—assisting with personal struggles

Tweedia—clearing sour thoughts

Veronica—traditions to be passed down

Viburnum (snowball)—encouragement

Willow, curly—flirtatiousness

Woollybush—clearing energy-zappers

Yarrow, cottage—honesty

Yarrow, tansy—removing negative personal thoughts

Yarrow, yellow—clearing negative people around you

# INDEX

Page numbers in **bold** refer to photographs.